THE *Lyric* LIB

T0040752

Love Songs

Complete Lyrics for 200 Songs

HAL•LEONARD®

Other books in *The Lyric Library*:

Broadway Volume I

Broadway Volume II

Christmas

Classic Rock

Contemporary Christian

Country

Early Rock 'n' Roll

Pop/Rock Ballads

ISBN 0-634-04459-1

Library of Congress cataloguing-in-publication data has been applied for.

Visit Hal Leonard Online at
www.halleonard.com

Preface

Songs have an uncanny ability to burrow deep into our gray matter, sometimes lying dormant for years or decades before something pings them back into our consciousness. All kinds of songs reside in there, more than we can count—not just songs we love and intentionally memorized and have sung again and again, but songs we once heard in passing, songs that form a soundtrack to significant people and places and moments in our lives, and even (or especially) songs that drive us crazy, like the chirping TV jingle that still won't let go years after the product it plugged has disappeared from the shelves.

Most of the time, though, our memories of songs are frustratingly incomplete unless we actively maintain them. The first verse and chorus that we blare out in the shower or at the jam session degenerates into mumbled lines, disconnected phrases, and bits and pieces inadvertently lifted from other songs. And, of course, there's the likelihood that what we *do* remember is riddled with mondegreens, or misheard lyrics. In these pages you'll find many opportunities to bring a little more completeness and accuracy to your repertoire of love songs, as well as to rediscover a nearly forgotten gem, wallow in nostalgia, or just browse through some prominent examples of the songwriter's craft.

The topic of love is, of course, the mother lode of songwriting—if love songs were summarily banned, radios and stereos around the world would fall mostly silent. Love songs are a place where intensely personal emotion strikes a universal chord; songwriter, singer, and listener all imagine themselves as the "I" or "you" of the lyrics, dreaming of love, reveling in love, watching love slip away, wistfully recalling some long-ago flowering of love.

The full arc of modern pop songwriting can be traced through the selections in this book, from the suave sophistication of Cole Porter, Irving Berlin, Howard Arlen, et al., through Motown and the Beatles and Stevie Wonder and beyond. Reading over these words will undoubtedly evoke the great voices who serenaded us with them (Elvis Presley, Frank Sinatra, Ella Fitzgerald, Dionne Warwick...), but many of these songs have lived long enough to be revisited by several generations of performers. When a songwriter truly captures a moment or mood of love—"the first time ever I saw your face"—we can't help but submit, time and time again.

Contents

Love Songs

All My Loving

Words and Music by John Lennon and Paul McCartney

from the film *A Hard Day's Night*
recorded by The Beatles

Close your eyes and I'll kiss you,
Tomorrow I'll miss you;
Remember I'll always be true.
And then while I'm away,
I'll write home everyday,
And I'll send all my loving to you.

I'll pretend that I'm kissing,
The lips I am missing
And hope that my dreams will come true.
And then while I'm away,
I'll write home everyday,
And I'll send all my loving to you.

All my loving,
I will send to you,
All my loving,
Darling, I'll be true.

Repeat Song

All my loving,
All my loving, oo,
All my loving
I will send to you.

All of You

Words and Music by Cole Porter

from the musical *Silk Stockings*
recorded by Fred Astaire and various other artists

I love the looks of you, the lure of you.
The sweet of you, the pure of you.
The eyes, the arms, the mouth of you.
The east, west, north and the south of you.
I'd love to gain complete control of you.
And handle even the heart and soul of you.
So love, at least, a small percent of me do.
For I love all of you.

Alternate Verse:
I love the looks of you, the lure of you.
I'd love to make a tour of you.
The eyes, the arms, the mouth of you.
The east, west, north, and the south of you.
I'd love to gain complete control of you.
And handle even the heart and soul of you.
So love, at least, a small percent of me, do.
For I love all of you.

Always

Words and Music by Irving Berlin

dropped from the musical The Cocoanuts
a standard recorded by various artists

Everything went wrong
And the whole day long
I'd feel so blue.
For the longest while
I'd forget to smile.
Then I met you.

Now that my blue days have passed,
Now that I've found you at last,
I'll be loving you, always
With a love that's true, always
When the things you've planned
Need a helping hand,
I will understand, always,
Always.

Days may not be fair, always.
That's when I'll be there, always,
Not for just an hour,
Not for just a day,
Not for just a year, but
Always.

Dreams will all come true,
Growing old with you,
And time will fly,
Caring each day more
Than the day before,
Till spring rolls by.

Then when the springtime has gone,
Then will my love linger on.
I'll be loving you, always
With a love that's true, always
When the things you've planned
Need a helping hand,
I will understand, always,
Always.

Days may not be fair, always.
That's when I'll be there, always,
Not for just an hour,
Not for just a day,
Not for just a year, but
Always.

Always in My Heart (Siempre en mi corazón)

Music and Spanish Words by Ernesto Lecuona
English Words by Kim Gannon

from the film *Always in My Heart*
a standard recorded by various artists

You are always in my heart,
Even though you're far away.
I can hear the music
Of the song of love I sang with you.
You are always in my heart,
And when skies above are gray,
I remember that you care,
And then and there the sun breaks through.

Just before I go to sleep,
There's a rendezvous I keep,
And the dreams I always meet
Help me forget we're far apart.
I don't know exactly when dear,
But I'm sure we'll meet again, dear,
And my darling 'til we do,
You are always in my heart.

And I Love Her

Words and Music by John Lennon and Paul McCartney

from the film *A Hard Day's Night*
recorded by The Beatles

I give her all my love,
That's all I do.
And if you saw my love,
You'd love her too.
I love her.

She gives me everything,
And tenderly.
The kiss my lover brings,
She brings to me.
And I love her.

A love like ours
Could never die,
As long as I
Have you near me.

Twice:
Bright are the stars that shine,
Dark is the sky.
I know this love of mine
Will never die.
And I love her.

Anniversary Song

By Al Jolson and Saul Chaplin

from the Columbia Picture *The Jolson Story*

Oh, how we danced on the night we were wed.
We vowed our true love, though a word wasn't said.
The world was in bloom, there were stars in the skies,
Except for the few that were there in your eyes.

Dear, as I held you so close in my arms,
Angels were singing a hymn to your charms.
Two hearts gently beating were murmuring low,
"My darling, I love you so."

The night seemed to fade into blossoming dawn.
The sun shone anew but the dance lingered on.
Could we but relive that sweet moment sublime,
We'd find that our love is unaltered by time.

The Anniversary Waltz

Words and Music by Al Dubin and Dave Franklin

We just discovered each other
Tonight when the lights were low;
One dance led up to another,
And now I can't let you go, so,

Tell me I may always dance
The anniversary waltz with you.
Tell me this is real romance,
An anniversary dream come true.
Let this be the anthem to our future years,
To millions of smiles and a few little tears.
May I always listen to
The anniversary waltz with you.

Baby, Come to Me

Words and Music by Rod Temperton

recorded by James Ingram & Patti Austin

Thinkin' back in time,
When love was only in the mind,
I realize ain't no second chance;
You've got to hold on to romance.
Don't let it slide.
There's a special kind of magic in the air
When you find another heart that needs
   to share.

Refrain:
Baby, come to me;
Let me put my arms around you.
This was meant to be,
And I'm oh, so glad I found you.
Need you every day;
Got to have your love around me.
Baby, always stay,
'Cause I can't go back to livin' without you.

Spendin' every dime
To keep you talkin' on the line;
That's how it was,
And all those walks together out in any kind
   of weather,
Just because.
There's a brand new way of looking
   at your life,
When you know that love is standing
   by your side.

Refrain

The night can get cold;
There's a chill to every evening when you're
   all alone.
Don't talk anymore,
'Cause you know that I'll be here to keep you
   warm.

Refrain

Baby, It's Cold Outside

By Frank Loesser

from the Motion Picture *Neptune's Daughter*
a standard recorded by various artists

*Note: The song is a duet; the male lines are in
parentheses*

I really can't stay,
(But baby it's cold outside!)
I've got to go 'way.
(But baby it's cold outside!)
This evening has been
(Been hoping that you'd drop in!)
So very nice.
(I'll hold your hands they're just like ice.)
My mother will start to worry
(Beautiful, what's your hurry?)
And father will be pacing the floor.
(Listen to the fireplace roar!)
So really I'd better scurry,
(Beautiful, please don't hurry.)
Well, maybe just half a drink more.
(Put some records on while I pour.)
The neighbors might think
(But, baby it's bad out there.)
Say, what's in the drink?
(No cabs to be had out there.)
I wish I knew how
(Your eyes are like starlight now)
To break the spell.
(I'll take your hat your hair looks swell.)
I ought to say "No, no, no, Sir!"
(Mind if I move in closer?)
At least I'm gonna say that I tried.
(What's the sense of hurting my pride.)
I really can't stay
(Oh, baby, don't hold out,)
Ah, but it's cold outside.
(Baby, it's cold outside.)

I simply must go.
(But baby it's cold outside!)
The answer is no!
(But baby it's cold outside!)
The welcome has been,
(How lucky that you dropped in!)
So nice and warm.
(Look out the window at that storm.)
My sister will be suspicious,
(Gosh, your lips look delicious.)
My brother will be there at the door.
(Waves upon a tropical shore!)
My maiden aunt's mind is vicious.
(Gosh, your lips are delicious)
Well, maybe just a cigarette more.
(Never such a blizzard before.)
I've got to get home
(But, baby, you'd freeze out there)
Say, lend me a comb.
(It's up to your knees out there.)

You've really been grand,
(I thrill when you touch my hand)
But don't you see.
(How can you do this thing to me.)
There's bound to be talk tomorrow.
(Think of my life-long sorrow.)
At least there will be plenty implied.
(If you caught pneumonia and died.)
I really can't stay
(Get over that old doubt,)
Ah, but it's cold outside.
(Baby, it's cold outside.)

Beautiful in My Eyes

Words and Music by Joshua Kadison

recorded by Joshua Kadison

You're my peace of mind
In this crazy world.
You're everything I've tried to find.
Your love is a pearl.
You're my Mona Lisa,
   you're my rainbow skies,
And my only prayer is that you realize,
You'll always be beautiful in my eyes.

The world will turn
And the seasons will change,
And all the lessons we will learn
Will be beautiful and strange.
We'll have our fill of tears,
   our share of sighs.
My only prayer is that you realize,
You'll always be beautiful in my eyes.

You will always be beautiful in my eyes.
And the passing years will show
That you will always grow,
Ever more beautiful in my eyes.

When there are lines upon my face,
From a lifetime of smiles.
When the time comes to embrace
For one long last while;
We can laugh about how time really flies.
We won't say goodbye 'cause
   true love never dies;
You'll always be beautiful in my eyes.

You'll always be beautiful in my eyes.
And the passing years will show
That you will always grow,
Ever more beautiful in my eyes.

The passing years will show
That you will always grow,
More beautiful in my eyes.

Beyond the Sea

English Lyrics by Jack Lawrence
Music and French Lyrics by Charles Trenet

recorded by Bobby Darin and various other artists

Somewhere beyond the sea,
Somewhere waiting for me,
My lover stands on golden sands
And watches the ships that go sailing.

Somewhere beyond the sea,
He's (She's) there watching for me.
If I could fly like birds on high,
Then straight to his (her) arms

I'd go sailing.
It's far beyond a star;
It's near beyond the moon.
I know beyond a doubt,
My heart will lead me there soon.

We'll meet beyond the shore:
We'll kiss just as before.
Happy we'll be beyond the sea,
And never again I'll go sailing.

Both to Each Other (Friends and Lovers)

Words and Music by Paul Gordon and Jay Gruska

recorded by Gloria Loring & Carl Anderson

What would you say if I told you
I've always wanted to hold you?
I don't know what we're afraid of;
Nothing would change if we made love.

Refrain:
'Cause I'll be your friend, and I'll be your lover.
Well, I know in our hearts we agree
We don't have to be one or the other.
No, we could be both to each other.

Yes, it's a chance that we're taking,
And somebody's heart may be breaking.
But we can't stop what's inside us;
Our love for each other will guide us.

Refrain

I've been through you and you've been through me.
Sometimes a friend is the hardest to see.
And we always know when it's laid on the line.
Nobody else is as easy to find.

So I'll be your friend, and I'll be your lover.
Well, I know in our hearts we agree
We don't have to be one or the other.
No, we could be both to each other.

But Beautiful

Words by Johnny Burke
Music by Jimmy Van Heusen

a standard recorded by various artists

Love is funny or it's sad,
Or it's quiet or it's mad;
It's a good thing or it's bad,
But beautiful!
Beautiful to take a chance,
And if you fall, you fall.
And I'm thinkin'
I wouldn't mind at all.

Love is tearful or it's gay;
It's a problem or it's play;
It's a heartache either way,
But beautiful!
And I'm thinkin'
If you were mine,
I'd never let you go,
And that would be but beautiful I know.

C'est Magnifique

Words and Music by Cole Porter

from the musical *Can-Can*
recorded by Frank Sinatra and Shirley MacLaine and various other artists

Love is such a fantastic affair,
When it comes to call,
After taking you up in the air,
Down it lets you fall.
But be patient and soon you will find,
If you follow your heart, not your mind,
Love is waiting there, again,
To take you up in the air, again.

Refrain:
When love comes in,
And takes you for a spin,
Oo-la-la-la,
C'est magnifique.
When ev'ry night
Your loved one holds you tight,
Oo-la-la-la,
C'est magnifique.
But when, one day,
Your loved one drifts away,
Oo-la-la-la,
It is so tragique.
But when, once more,
He [She] whispers,
"Je t'adore,"
C'est magnifique.

Refrain

Additional Lyrics
Verse 2:
When you began of love to speak,
I followed every word.
But when you called love magnifique,
I would have called it absurd.
And when you said it was often tragique,
I would have said it was always comique.
So, mad'moiselle, be sweet to me,
And kindly do not repeat to me.

Call Me Irresponsible

Words by Sammy Cahn
Music by James Van Heusen

cut from an abandoned Fred Astaire film
from the Paramount Picture *Papa's Delicate Condition*
a standard recorded by Frank Sinatra, Jack Jones and various other artists

Call me irresponsible,
Call me unreliable,
Throw in undependable too.

Do my foolish alibis bore you?
Well, I'm not too clever.
I just adore you.

Call me unpredictable,
Tell me I'm impractical,
Rainbows I'm inclined to pursue.

Call me irresponsible,
Yes, I'm unreliable,
But it's undeniably true,
I'm irresponsibly mad for you!

Can You Feel the Love Tonight

Music by Elton John
Lyrics by Tim Rice

from Walt Disney Pictures' *The Lion King*
recorded by Elton John

There's a calm surrender
To the rush of the day,
When the heat of the rolling world
Can be turned away.
An enchanted moment,
And it sees me through.
It's enough for this restless warrior
Just to be with you.

Refrain:
And can you feel the love tonight?
It is where we are.
It's enough for this wide-eyed wanderer
That we got this far.
And can you feel the love tonight,
How it's laid to rest?
It's enough to make kings and vagabonds
Believe the very best.

There's a time for everyone,
If they only learn,
That the twisting kaleidoscope
Moves us all in turn.
There's a rhyme and reason
To the wild outdoors,

When the heart of this star-crossed voyager
Beats in time with yours.

Refrain

Candle on the Water

Words and Music by Al Kasha and Joel Hirschhorn

from Walt Disney's *Pete's Dragon*
recorded by Helen Reddy

I'll be your candle on the water,
My love for you will always burn.
I know you're lost and drifting,
But the clouds are lifting,
Don't give up, you have somewhere to turn.

I'll be your candle on the water,
'Til every wave is warm and bright,
My soul is there beside you,
Let this candle guide you,
Soon you'll see a golden stream of light.

A cold and friendless tide has found you,
Don't let the stormy darkness pull you down.
I'll paint a ray of hope around you,
Circling in the air lighted by a prayer.

I'll be your candle on the water,
This flame inside of me will grow.
Keep holding on, you'll make it,
Here's my hand so take it,
Look for me reaching out to show
As sure as rivers flow,
I'll never let you go,
I'll never let you go.
I'll never let you go.

Change Partners

Words and Music by Irving Berlin

from the RKO Radio Motion Picture *Carefree*
recorded by Fred Astaire and various other artists

Must you dance every dance
With the same fortunate man?
You have danced with him since the music began.
Won't you change partners and dance with me?

Must you dance quite so close
With your lips touching his face?
Can't you see I'm longing to be in his place?
Won't you change partners and dance with me?

Ask him to sit this one out,
And while you're alone
I'll tell the waiter to tell him
He's wanted on the telephone.

You've been locked in his arms
Ever since heaven knows when.
Won't you change partners, and then
You may never want to change partners again.

Cheek to Cheek

Words and Music by Irving Berlin

from the RKO Radio Motion Picture *Top Hat*
a standard recorded by Fred Astaire and various other artists

Heaven, I'm in heaven.
And my heart beats so that I can hardly speak.
And I seem to find the happiness I seek
When we're out together dancing cheek to cheek.

Heaven, I'm in heaven.
And the cares that hung around me through the week
Seem to vanish like a gambler's lucky streak
When we're out together dancing cheek to cheek.

Oh, I love to climb a mountain,
And to reach the highest peak.
But it doesn't thrill me half as much
As dancing cheek to cheek.

Oh I love to go out fishing
In a river or a creek
But I don't enjoy it half as much
As dancing cheek to cheek.

Dance with me.
I want my arm about you.
The charm about you
Will carry me through to

Heaven, I'm in heaven.
And my heart beats so that I can hardly speak.
And I seem to find the happiness I seek
When we're out together
Dancing cheek to cheek.

(They Long to Be) Close to You

Lyric by Hal David
Music by Burt Bacharach

recorded by The Carpenters

Why do birds
Suddenly appear
Every time
You are near?
Just like me
They long to be
Close to you.
Why do stars
Fall down from the sky
Every time
You walk by?
Just like me
They long to be
Close to you.

On the day that you were born
The angels got together
And decided to create a dream come true.
So they sprinkled moon-dust in your hair
And gold and starlight in your eyes of blue.

That is why
All the boys (girls) in town
Follow you all around.
Just like me
They long to be
Close to you.

Just like me
They long to be
Close to you.

The Colour of My Love

Words and Music by David Foster and Arthur Janov

from the musical *Scream*
recorded by Celine Dion

I'll paint my mood in shades of blue,
Paint my soul to be with you.
I'll sketch your lips in shaded tones,
Draw your mouth to my own.

I'll draw your arms around my waist
Then all doubt I shall erase.
I'll paint the rain that softly lands
On your windblown hair.

I'll trace a hand to wipe your tears,
A look to calm your fears,
A silhouette of dark and light
While we hold each other, oh, so tight.

I'll paint a sun to warm your heart,
Swearing that we'll never part.
That's the colour of my love.

I'll paint the truth, show how I feel,
Try to make you completely real.
I'll use a brush so light and fine
To draw you close and make you mine.

I'll paint a sun to warm your heart,
Swearing that we'll never, ever part.
That's the colour of my love.
I'll draw the years all passing by,

So much to learn, so much to try.
And with this ring our lives will start,
Swearing that we'll never part.
I offer what you cannot buy,
Devoted love until we die.

Come Rain or Come Shine

Words by Johnny Mercer
Music by Harold Arlen

from the musical *St. Louis Woman*
a standard recorded by various artists

I'm gonna love you like nobody's loved you,
Come rain or come shine.
High as the mountain and deep as the river,
Come rain or come shine.
I guess when you met me
It was just one of those things,
But don't ever bet me
'Cause I'm gonna be true if you let me.

You're gonna love me like nobody's loved me,
Come rain or come shine.
Happy together, unhappy together and won't it be fine.
Days may be cloudy or sunny.
We're in or we're out of the money,
But I'm with you always
I'm with you rain or shine.

Could I Have This Dance

Words and Music by Wayland Holyfield and Bob House

from the film *Urban Cowboy*
recorded by Anne Murray

I'll always remember
The song they were playing
The first time we danced and I knew.

And we swayed to the music
And held to each other,
I fell in love with you.

Refrain:
Could I have this dance for the rest of my life?
Would you be my partner every night?
When we're together it feels so right.
Could I have this dance for the rest of my life?

I'll always remember
That magic moment,
When I held you close to me.
As we moved together,
I knew forever you're all I'll ever need.
You're all I'll ever need.

Refrain

Darling, je vous aime beaucoup

Words and Music by Anna Sosenko

from the film *Love and Hisses*
recorded by Nat "King" Cole, Hildegarde and various other artists

An English boy in Paris
Fell for a lovely mademoiselle.
With no French at his command,
He tried to make her understand
He loved her more and more each day.
And in his own peculiar way,
He'd open up his heart and say:

Refrain:
Darling, je vous aime beaucoup,
Je ne sais pas what to do.
You know, you've completely stolen my heart.
Morning, noon, and nighttime too,
Toujours wond'ring what you do,
That's the way I've felt right from the start.
Ah, cherie! My love for you is très, très fort;
Wish my French were good enough,
I'd tell you so much more.
But I hope that you compree
All the things you mean to me.
Darling, je vous aime beaucoup,
I love you.

Repeat Refrain

Yes, I do.

Day by Day

Words and Music by Sammy Cahn, Axel Stordahl and Paul Weston

Theme from the Paramount Television Series *Day by Day*
a standard recorded by Frank Sinatra, Jo Stafford, Doris Day and various artists

Day by day,
I'm falling more in love with you,
And day by day
My love seems to grow.
There isn't any end to my devotion,
It's deeper, dear, by far, than any ocean.
I find that day by day
You're making all my dreams come true,
Do come what may,
I want you to know,
I'm yours alone,
And I'm in love to stay,
As we go through the years,
Day by day.

Dedicated to the One I Love

Words and Music by Lowman Pauling and Ralph Bass

recorded by The Shirelles, The Mamas and The Papas

While I'm far away from you, my baby,
I know it's hard for you, my baby,
Because it's hard for me, my baby.
And the darkest hour is just before dawn.
Each night before you go to bed, my baby,
Whisper a little prayer for me, my baby.
And then tell all the stars above.
This is dedicated to the one I love.

Life can never be exactly like I want it to be,
I could be satisfied knowing you love me.
There's one thing I want you to do especially for me,
And it's something that everybody needs.

While I'm far away from you, my baby,
Whisper a little prayer for me, my baby.
Because it's hard for me, my baby.
And the darkest hour is just before dawn.
There's one thing I want you to do especially for me,
And it's something everybody needs.

Each night before you go to bed, my baby,
Whisper a little prayer for me, my baby.
And then tell all the stars above.
This is dedicated to the one I love.

Repeat and Fade:
Dedicated to the one I love.
Dedicated to the one I love.

Don't Blame Me

Words by Dorothy Fields
Music by Jimmy McHugh

a standard recorded by various artists

Ever since the lucky night I found you
I've hung around you, just like a fool,
Falling head and heels in love like a kid out of school.
My poor heart is in an awful state now,
But it's too late now to call a halt,
So if I become a nuisance, it's all your fault!

Refrain:
Don't blame me for falling in love with you.
I'm under your spell but how can I help it,
Don't blame me.
Can't you see when you do the things you do,
If I can't conceal the thrill that I'm feeling,
Don't blame me.
I can't help it if that doggoned moon above
Makes me need someone like you to love.
Blame your kiss, as sweet as a kiss can be,
And blame all your charms that melt in my arms,
But don't blame me.

I like ev'ry single thing about you,
Without a doubt you are like a dream.
In my mind I find a picture of us as a team.
Ever since the hour of our meeting
I've been repeating a silly phrase,
Hoping that you'll understand me one of these days.

Refrain

Don't Know Much

Words and Music by Barry Mann, Cynthia Weil and Tom Snow

recorded by Linda Ronstadt & Aaron Neville

Look at this face,
I know the years are showing.
Look at this life,
I still don't know where it's going.

Refrain:
I don't know much,
But I know I love you,
And that may be
All I need to know.

Look at these eyes,
They've never seen what matters.
Look at these dreams,
So beaten and so battered.

Refrain

So many questions
Still left unanswered.
So much I've never broken through.
And when I feel you near me
Sometimes I see so clearly
The only truth I've ever known is me and you.

Look at this man,
So blessed with inspiration.
Look at this soul,
Still searching for salvation.

Refrain Twice

And that may be all there is to know.

Dream a Little Dream of Me

Words by Gus Kahn
Music by Wilbur Schwandt and Fabian Andree

recorded by Frankie Laine, Mama Cass and various other artists

Stars shining bright above you,
Night breezes seem to whisper, "I love you,"
Birds singing in the sycamore tree,
"Dream a little dream of me."

Say "Nightie-night" and kiss me,
Just hold me tight and tell me you'll miss me;
While I'm alone and blue as can be,
Dream a little dream of me.

Stars fading, but I linger on, dear,
Still craving your kiss;
I'm longing to linger till dawn, dear,
Just saying this:

Sweet dreams till sunbeams find you,
Sweet dreams that leave all worries behind you,
But in your dreams whatever they be,
Dream a little dream of me.

Easy to Love (You'd Be So Easy to Love)

Words and Music by Cole Porter

from *Born to Dance*
a standard recorded by various artists

You'd be so easy to love,
So easy to idolize all others above,
So worth the yearning for,
So swell to keep ev'ry home fire burning for.

We'd be so grand at the game,
So carefree together that it does seem a shame
That you can't see your future with me,
'Cause you'd be oh, so easy to love.

Endless Love

Words and Music by Lionel Richie

from the film *Endless Love*
recorded by Diana Ross & Lionel Richie; Mariah Carey & Luther Vandross

My love,
There's only you in my life,
The only thing that's right.
My first love,
You're every breath that I take,
You're every step I make.
And I,
I want to share all my love with you,
No one else
Will do.
And your eyes,
They tell me how much you care.
Oh yes,
You will always be
My endless love.

Two hearts,
Two hearts that beat as one,
Our lives have just begun.
Forever
I hold you close in my arms
I can't resist your charms.
And love,
I'd be a fool for you.
I'm sure you know
I don't mind,
'Cause you
You mean the world to me.
Oh I know
I found in you
My endless love.

Everything I Own

Words and Music by David Gates

recorded by Bread

You sheltered me from harm,
Kept me warm, kept me warm.
You gave my life to me, set me free.

The finest years I ever knew
Were all the years I had with you.
And I would give anything I own,
Give up my life, my heart, my home.
I would give everything I own
Just to have you back again.

You taught me how to love,
What it's of, what it's of.
You never said too much,
But still you showed the way,
And I knew from watching you.

Nobody else could ever know
The part of me that can't let go.
And I would give everything I own,
Give up my life, my heart, my home.
I would give everything I own
Just to have you back again.

Is there someone you know,
You're loving them so,
But taking them all for granted.
You may lose them one day,
Someone takes them away
And they don't hear the words
    you long to say.

And I would give everything
Give up my life, my heart, my home.
I would give everything I own
Just to have you back again.
Just to touch you once again.

Exactly Like You

Words by Dorothy Fields
Music by Jimmy McHugh

from the musical *International Revue*
featured in the musical *Sugar Babies*

I know why I've waited, know why I've been blue,
Prayed each night for someone exactly like you.
Why should we spend money on a show or two.
No one does those love scenes exactly like you.

You make me feel so grand.
I want to hand the world to you.
You seem to understand,
Each foolish little scheme I'm scheming,
Dream I'm dreaming.
Now I know why mother taught me to be true.
She meant me for someone exactly like you.

Fields of Gold

Written and Composed by G. M. Sumner

recorded by Sting

You'll remember me
When the west wind moves
Upon the fields of barley.
You'll forget the sun
In his jealous sky
As we walk in fields of gold.

So she took her love
For to gaze awhile
Upon the fields of barley.
In his arms she fell
As her hair came down
Among the fields of gold.

Will you stay with me,
Will you be my love
Among the fields of barley?
We'll forget the sun
In his jealous sky
As we lie in fields of gold.

See the west wind move
Like a lover so
Upon the fields of barley.
Feel her body rise
When you kiss her mouth
Among the fields of gold.
I never made promises lightly
And there have been some that I've broken,
But I swear in the days still left
We'll walk in fields of gold.
We'll walk in fields of gold.

Many years have passed
Since those summer days
Among the fields of barley.
See the children run
As the sun goes down
Among the fields of gold.

You'll remember me
When the west wind moves
Upon the fields of barley.
You can tell the sun
In his jealous sky
When we walked in fields of gold.
When we walked in fields of gold.

The First Time Ever I Saw Your Face

Words and Music by Ewan MacColl

recorded by Roberta Flack

The first time
Ever I saw your face,
I thought the sun
Rose in your eyes,
And the moon and the stars
Were the gifts you gave
To the dark
And the end of the skies.

The first time
Ever I kissed your mouth,
I felt the earth
Move in my hand,
Like the trembling heart
Of a captive bird
That was there
At my command,

The first time
Ever I lay with you
And felt your heart
So close to mine,
And I knew our joy
Would fill the earth
And last
Till the end of time,
My love.

The first time
Ever I saw
Your face.

Fly Me to the Moon (In Other Words)

Words and Music by Bart Howard

featured in the Motion Picture *Once Around*
a standard recorded by various artists

Fly me to the moon,
And let me play among the stars;
Let me see what spring
Is like on Jupiter and Mars.
In other words,
Hold my hand!
In other words
Darling, kiss me!

Fill my heart with song,
And let me sing forever more;
You are all I long for
All I worship and adore.
In other words,
Please be true.
In other words,
I love you!

For All We Know

Words by Sam M. Lewis
Music by J. Fred Coots

a standard recorded by various artists

Sweetheart, the night is growing old,
Sweetheart, my love is still untold,
A kiss that is never tasted
Forever and ever is wasted.

Refrain:
For all we know we may never meet again,
Before you go make this moment sweet again.
We won't say goodnight until the last minute;
I'll hold out my hand and my heart will be in it.
For all we know this may only be a dream;
We come and go like a ripple on a stream.
So love me tonight, tomorrow was made for some,
Tomorrow may never come, for all we know.

Why should we waste a night like this?
Why should we waste a single kiss?
Why can't we laugh at tomorrow?
Tomorrow will pay what we borrow.

Refrain

For Every Man There's a Woman

Lyric by Leo Robin
Music by Harold Arlen

from the Motion Picture *Casbah*
a standard recorded by various artists

For ev'ry man there's a woman,
For ev'ry life there's a plan,
And wise men know it was ever so.
Since the world began,
Woman was made for man.
Where is she, where is the woman for me?

For ev'ry prince there's a princess,
For ev'ry Joe there's a Joan,
And if you wait, you will meet the mate
Born for you alone,
Happy to be your own.
Where is she, where is the woman for me?

Find the one, find the one,
Then together you will find the sun.

For ev'ry heart there's a moment,
For ev'ry hand, a glove,
And for ev'ry woman, a man to love.

Repeat All

Where is she, where is the one for me?

For Once in My Life

Words by Ronald Miller
Music by Orlando Murden

recorded by Stevie Wonder

Goodbye, old friend,
This is the end
Of the man I used to be.
'Cause there's been a strange
And welcome change in me.

For once in my life I have someone who needs me,
Someone I've needed so long.
For once, unafraid I can go where life leads me
And somehow I know I'll be strong.
For once I can touch what my heart used to dream of
Long before I knew.
Someone warm like you
Would make my dream come true.
For once in my life
I won't let sorrow hurt me, not like it's hurt me before.
For once I have something I know won't desert me,
I'm not alone anymore.
For once I can say this is mine, you can't take it,
Long as I know I have love, I can make it.

First Time:
For once in my life
I have someone who needs me.
Repeat Song

Second Time:
For once I can feel
That somebody's heard my plea.
For once in my life
I have someone who needs me.

Gentle on My Mind

Words and Music by John Hartford

recorded by Glen Campbell

It's knowing that your door is always open,
And your path is free to walk,
That makes me tend to leave my sleeping bag,
Rolled up and stashed behind your couch.

And it's knowing I'm not shackled,
By forgotten words and bonds,
And the ink stains that have dried upon some line;
That keeps you in the back-roads
By the rivers of my memory,
That keeps you gentle on my mind.

The Gift

Words and Music by Tom Douglas and Jim Brickman

recorded by Jim Brickman featuring Collin Raye and Susan Ashton

Female:
Winter snow is falling down,
Children laughing all around,
Lights are turning on,
Like a fairy tale come true.
Sitting by the fire we made,
You're the answer when I prayed
I would find someone
And baby, I found you.

All I want is to hold you forever.
All I need is you more every day.
You saved my heart from being
  broken apart.
You gave your love away,
And I'm thankful every day for the gift.

Male:
Watching as you softly sleep,
What I'd give if I could keep
Just this moment,
If only time stood still.
But the colors fade away,
And the years will make us gray,
But, baby, in my eyes, you'll still
  be beautiful.

Both:
All I want is to hold you forever.
All I need is you more every day.

Male:
You saved my heart from being
  broken apart.

Female:
You gave your love away.

Male:
And I'm thankful every day.

Both:
For the gift.

Both:
All I want is to hold you forever.
All I need is you more every day.

Male:
You saved my heart from being
  broken apart.

Female:
You gave your love away.

Male:
I can't find the words to say.

Female:
That I'm thankful every day.

Both:
For the gift.

The Girl That I Marry

Words and Music by Irving Berlin

from the Stage Production *Annie Get Your Gun*

The girl that I marry will have to be
As soft and as pink as a nursery.
The girl I call my own,
Will wear satin and laces and smell of cologne.

Her nails will be polished and in her hair,
She'll wear a gardenia. And I'll be there
'Stead of flittin' I'll be sittin'
Next to her and she'll purr like a kitten.

A doll I can carry,
The girl that I marry must be.

The Glory of Love

Words and Music by Billy Hill

a standard recorded by various artists
featured in the films *Guess Who's Coming to Dinner?* and *Beaches*

You've got to give a little, take a little
And let your heart break a little,
That's the story of,
That's the glory of love.

You've got to laugh a little,
Cry a little,
Before the clouds roll by a little,
That's the story of,
That's the glory of love.

As long as there's the two of us
We've got the world and all its charms,
And when the world is through with us
We've got each other's arms.

You've got to win a little,
Lose a little,
And always have the blues a little,
That's the story of,
That's the glory of love.

A Groovy Kind of Love

Words and Music by Toni Wine and Carole Bayer Sager

recorded by The Mindbenders, Phil Collins

When I'm feelin' blue,
All I have to do
Is take a look at you,
Then I'm not so blue.
When you're close to me
I can feel your heart beat
I can hear you breathing in my ear.

Refrain:
Wouldn't you agree,
Baby, you and me
Got a groovy kind of love.
We got a groovy kind of love.

Anytime you want to
You can turn me on to
Anything you want to,
Any time at all.
When I taste your lips,
Oh, I start to shiver,
Can't control the quivering inside.

Refrain

When I'm in your arms
Nothing seems to matter
If the world would shatter
I don't care.

Refrain

Grow Old with Me

Words and Music by John Lennon

recorded by John Lennon, Mary Chapin Carpenter

Grow old along with me.
The best is yet to be,
When our time has come,
We will be as one.

Refrain:
God bless our love,
God bless our love.

Grow old along with me.
Two branches of one tree,
Face the setting sun,
When the day is done.

Refrain

Spending our lives together,
Man and wife together,
World without end,
World without end.

Grow old along with me.
Whatever fate decrees,
We will see it through,
For our love is true.

Refrain

The Hawaiian Wedding Song (Ke kali nei au)

English Lyrics by Al Hoffman and Dick Manning
Hawaiian Lyrics and Music by Charles E. King

recorded by Elvis Presley, Andy Williams

This is the moment I've waited for.
I can hear my heart singing,
Soon bells will be ringing.
This is the moment of sweet aloha,
I will love you longer than forever,
Promise that you will leave me never.
Here and now, dear,
All my love I vow, dear,
Promise me that you will leave me never,
I will love you longer than forever.
Now that we are one, clouds won't
   hide the sun.
Blue skies of Hawaii smile on this,
   our wedding day.
I do love you with all my heart.

Hawaiian Lyric:
Eia au ke kali nei
Aia la i hea kuu aloha
Eia au ke huli nei
A loaa oe e ka ipo
Maha ka iini a ka puuwai
Ua sila' paa ia me oe
Ko aloha makamae e ipo
Ka 'u ia e lei ae neila
Nou no ka iini
A nou wale no
A o ko aloha ka'u e hiipoi mau
Na'u oe nau'u oe, e lei e lei
Na'u oe e lei

A he halia kai hiki mai
No kuu lei onaona
Pulupe i ka ua
Auhea oe kaiini a loko
Nu loko ae ka manao
Hu'e luni ana i kuu kino
Kuu pua kuu lei onaona
A'u i kui a lawai a nei
Me ke ala pua pikake
A o oe kuu pua
Ku'u pua lei lehua
A'u e li'a mau nei hoopaa
Ia iho kealoha
He lei, he lei, oe na'u, oe na'u
He lei 'oe na'u

Heart and Soul

Words by Frank Loesser
Music by Hoagy Carmichael

from the Paramount Short Subject *A Song Is Born*
a standard recorded by Eddy Duchin, Johnny Maddox,
The Cleftones, Jan & Dean and various other artists

I've let a pair of arms enslave me oft time before,
But more than just a thrill you gave me,
Yes more, much more.

Heart and soul,
I fell in love with you.
Heart and soul,
The way a fool would do
Madly,
Because you held me tight
And stole a kiss in the night.

Heart and soul,
I begged to be adored.
Lost control
And tumbled overboard
Gladly
That magic night we kissed
There in the moon-mist.

Oh! But your lips were thrilling, much too thrilling.
Never before were mine so strangely willing.

But now I see
What one embrace can do.
Look at me,
It's got me loving you
Madly;
That little kiss you stole
Held all my heart and soul.

Hello, Young Lovers

Lyrics by Oscar Hammerstein II
Music by Richard Rodgers

from the musical *The King and I*

When I think of Tom
I think about a night
When the earth smelled of summer
And the sky was streaked with white,
And the soft mist of England
Was sleeping on a hill,
I remember this
And I always will.
There are new lovers now
On the same silent hill
Looking on the same blue sea,
And I know Tom and I
Are a part of them all
And they're all a part of Tom and me.

Hello, young lovers,
Whoever you are,
I hope your troubles are few
All my good wishes go with you tonight
I've been in love like you.
Be brave, young lovers,
  and follow your star,
Be brave and faithful and true.
Cling very close to each other tonight
I've been in love like you.

I know how it feels
To have wings on your heels,
And to fly down a street in a trance
You fly down a street
On a chance that you'll meet,
And you meet
Not really by chance.

Don't cry young lovers,
Whatever you do,
Don't cry because I'm alone.
All of my memories are happy tonight!
I've had a love of my own,
I've had a love of my own like yours,
I've had a love of my own.

Here and Now

Words and Music by Terry Steele and David Elliot

recorded by Luther Vandross

One look in your eyes,
And there I see
Just what you mean to me.
Here in my heart I believe
Your love is all I ever need.
Holding you close through the night,
I need you. Yeah.

I look in your eyes and there I see
What happiness really means.
The love that we share makes life so sweet.
Together we'll always be.
This pledge of love feels so right,
And ooh, I need you. Yeah.

Refrain:
Here and now,
I promise to love faithfully.
You're all I need.
Here and now,
I vow to be one with thee.
Your love is all I need.

Stay.

When I look in your eyes
And there I see
All that a love should really be.
And I need you more and more each day.
Nothing can take your love away.
More than I dare to dream.
I need you.

Refrain

Starting here.
Ooh, and I'm starting now.
I believe (I believe)
Starting here.
I'm starting right here.
Starting now.
Right now because I believe in your love,
So I'm glad to take the vow.
Here and now, oh,
I promise to love you faithfully.
You're all I need.
Here and now,
I vow to be one with thee.
Your love is all I need.

Here, There and Everywhere

Words and Music by John Lennon and Paul McCartney

recorded by The Beatles

To lead a better life
I need my love to be here.

Here, making each day of the year,
Changing my life with a wave of her hand.
Nobody can deny that there's something there.
There, running my hands through her hair,
Both of us thinking how good it can be.
Someone is speaking, but she doesn't know he's there.

Refrain:
I want her everywhere
And if she's beside me I know I need never care.
But to love her is to need her everywhere,
Knowing that love is to share;
Each one believing that love never dies,
Watching her and hoping I'm always there.

Repeat Refrain

I will be there
And everywhere,
Here, there and everywhere.

How Deep Is the Ocean (How High Is the Sky)

Words and Music by Irving Berlin

a standard recorded by Bing Crosby, Coleman Hawkins, Peggy Lee,
Artie Shaw, Frank Sinatra and various other artists

How much do I love you?
I'll tell you no lie,
How deep is the ocean,
How high the sky?

How many times a day do I think of you?
How many roses are sprinkled with dew?

How far would I travel
To be where you are?
How far is the journey
From here to a star?

And if I ever lost you,
How much would I cry?
How deep is the ocean,
How high the sky?

How Deep Is Your Love

Words and Music by Barry Gibb, Maurice Gibb and Robin Gibb

from the Motion Picture *Saturday Night Fever*
recorded by The Bee Gees

I know your eyes in the morning sun.
I feel you touch me in the pouring rain.
And the moment that you wander far from me,
I wanna feel you in my arms again.
And you come to me on a summer breeze;
Keep me warm in your love,
Then you softly leave.

Refrain:
And it's me you need to show
How deep is your love?
How deep is your love?
How deep is your love?
I really mean to learn.
'Cause we're living in a world of fools,
Breaking us down
When they all should let us be.
We belong to you and me.

I believe in you.
You know the door to my very soul.
You're the light in my deepest, darkest hour;
You're my savior when I fall.
And you may not think I care for you
When you know down inside
That I really do.

Refrain

How High the Moon

Words by Nancy Hamilton
Music by Morgan Lewis

from the musical *Two for the Show*
a standard recorded by Benny Goodman, Les Paul and Mary Ford,
Ella Fitzgerald and various other artists

Somewhere there's music,
How faint the tune!
Somewhere there's heaven,
How high the moon!
There is no moon above
When love is far away too,
Till it comes true
That you love me as I love you.

Somewhere's there's music,
It's where you are,
Somewhere there's heaven,
How near, how far!
The darkest night would shine
If you would come to me soon,
Until you will,
How still my heart,
How high the moon!

How Sweet It Is (To Be Loved by You)

Words and Music by Edward Holland, Lamont Dozier and Brian Holland

recorded by Marvin Gaye, James Taylor

Refrain:
How sweet it is to be loved by you.
How sweet it is to be loved by you.

I needed the shelter of someone's arms,
There you were.
I needed someone to understand my ups and downs,
There you were.
With sweet love and devotion,
Deeply touching my emotion.
I want to stop and thank you, baby;
I want to stop and thank you, baby, yes I do.

Refrain

I close my eyes at night,
Wonderin' where would I be without you in my life.
Ev'rything I did was just a bore,
Ev'rywhere I went, seems I've been there before.
But you brighten up for me all of my days
With a love so sweet in so many ways.
I want to stop and thank you, baby;
I want to stop and thank you, baby, yes I do.

Refrain

You were better to me than I was to myself.
For me there's you and there ain't nobody else.
I want to stop and thank you, baby;
I want to stop and thank you, baby, yes I do.

Refrain

I Believe

Words and Music by Jeffrey Pence, Eliot Sloan and Matt Senatore

recorded by Blessid Union of Souls

Walk blindly to the light and
   reach out for his hand.
Don't ask any question and
   don't try to understand.
Open up your mind and
   then open up your heart,
And you will see that you and me
   aren't very far apart.

'Cause I believe that love is the answer.
I believe that love will find a way.

Violence has spread worldwide and
   there's fam'lies on the street.
We sell drugs to children now.
   Oh, why can't we just see
That all we do is eliminate our future
   with things we do today?
Money is our incentive now,
   so that makes it okay.

But I believe that love is the answer.
I believe that love will find a way.
I believe that love is the answer.
I believe love will find a way.

I've been seeing Lisa now for
   a little over a year.
She says she'd never been so happy,
   but Lisa lives in fear
That one day daddy's gonna find out she's in
   love with a nigger from the streets.
Oh, how he would lose it then,
   but she's still here with me.

'Cause she believes that love will see it
   through and they'll understand.
He'll see me as a person and
   not just a black man.
'Cause I believe that love is the answer.
I believe that love will find a way.
I believe, I believe, I believe,
   I believe that love is the answer.
I believe love will find a way.
Love will find a way.
Love will find a way.
Love will find a way.

I Believe in You and Me

Words and Music by David Wolfert and Sandy Linzer

from the Touchstone Motion Picture *The Preacher's Wife*
recorded by Whitney Houston

I believe in you and me.
I believe that we will be
In love eternally.
Well, as far as I can see,
You will always be
The one for me,
Oh, yes, you will.

And I believe in dreams again.
I believe that love will never end.
And like the river finds the sea,
I was lost, now I'm free
'Cause I believe in you and me.

I will never leave your side.
I will never hurt your pride.
When all the chips are down,
Babe, then I will always be around.
Just to be right where you are, my love.
You know I love you, boy.
I'll never leave you out.
I will always let you in, boy,
Oh, baby, to places no one's ever been.
Deep inside, can't you see
That I believe in you and me.

Maybe I'm a fool to feel the way I do.
I would play the fool forever
Just to be with you forever.
I believe in miracles
And love's a miracle,
And yes, baby, you're my dream come true.
I, I was lost, now I'm free,
Oh baby,
'Cause
I believe, I do believe in you and me.
See, I'm lost, now I'm free
'Cause I believe in you and me.

I Can Dream, Can't I?

Lyric by Irving Kahal
Music by Sammy Fain

from the musical *Right This Way*
a standard recorded by various artists

I can see, no matter how near you'll be,
You'll never belong to me.
But I can dream, can't I?
Can't I pretend that I'm locked in the bend of your embrace?
For dreams are just like wine,
And I am drunk with mine.

I'm aware my heart is a sad affair.
There's much disillusion there,
But I can dream, can't I?
Can't I adore you although we are oceans apart?
I can't make you open your heart,
But I can dream, can't I?

I Concentrate on You

Words and Music by Cole Porter

from the film *Broadway Melody of 1940*

Whenever skies look gray to me
And trouble begins to brew,
Whenever the winter winds
Become too strong,
I concentrate on you.

When fortune cries "nay, nay!" to me
And people declare "You're through."
Whenever the blues become
My only song,
I concentrate on you.

On your smile so sweet, so tender,
When at first my {your} kiss you {I} decline,
On the light in your eyes,
When you {I} surrender
And once again our arms intertwine.

And so when wise men say to me
That love's young dream never comes true,
To prove that even wise men can be wrong,
I concentrate on you.
I concentrate,
And concentrate
On you.

I Don't Want to Set the World on Fire

Words and Music by Sol Marcus, Bennie Benjamin and Eddie Seiler

a standard recorded by The Ink Spots, Donna Wood, The Don Juans and various other artists

I don't want to set the world on fire,
I just want to start
A flame in your heart.
In my heart I have but one desire,
And that one is you
No other will do.

I've lost all ambition
For worldly acclaim,
I just want to be the one you love;
And with your admission
That you feel the same
I'll have reached the goal I'm dreaming of.
Believe me!

I don't want to set the world on fire,
I just want to start
A flame in your heart.

I Finally Found Someone

Words and Music by Barbra Streisand, Marvin Hamlisch, R.J. Lange and Bryan Adams

from the film *The Mirror Has Two Faces*
recorded by Barbra Streisand & Bryan Adams

He: I finally found someone
Who knocks me off my feet.
I finally found someone
Who makes me feel complete.

She: It started over coffee.
We started out as friends.
It's funny how from simple things
The best things begin.

He: This time it's different.
It's all because of you.
It's better than it's ever been
'Cause we can talk it through.

She: My favorite line
Was, "Can I call you sometime?"
It's all you had to say
To take my breath away.

Both: This is it,
Oh, I finally found someone,
Someone to share my life.
I finally found the one
To be with every night.

She: 'Cause whatever I do,
He: It's just got to be you.

Both: My life has just begun.
I finally found someone.

He: Did I keep you waiting?
She: I didn't mind.
He: I apologize.
She: Baby, that's fine.
He: I would wait forever
Both: Just to know you were mine.
He: You know, I love your hair
She: Are you sure it looks right?
He: I love what you wear.
She: Isn't it too tight?
He: You're exceptional.
Both: I can't wait for the rest of my life.

This is it.
Oh, I finally found someone,
Someone to share my life.
I finally found someone
To be with every night.

She: 'Cause whatever I do,
He: It's just got to be you.

Both: My life has just begun.
I finally found someone.

She: And whatever I do,
He: It's just got to be you.
She: My life has just begun.
Both: I finally found someone.

I Honestly Love You

Words and Music by Peter Allen and Jeff Barry

recorded by Olivia Newton-John

Maybe I hang around here a little more than I should.
We both know I got somewhere else to go.
But I got somethin' to tell you that I never thought I would,
But I believe you really ought to know.
I love you.
I honestly love you.

You don't have to answer, I see it in your eyes.
Maybe it was better left unsaid.
But this is pure and simple and you must realize,
That it's comin' from my heart and not my head.
I love you.
I honestly love you.

I'm not tryin' to make you feel uncomfortable
I'm not tryin' to make you anything at all.
But this feeling doesn't come along every day,
And you shouldn't blow the chance,
When you've got the chance to say:
I love you.
Spoken:
I love you.
Sung:
I honestly love you.

If we both were born in another place and time,
This moment might be ending with a kiss.
But there you are with yours and here I am with mine,
So I guess we'll just be leaving it at this:
I love you.
I honestly love you.
I honestly love you.

I Just Called to Say I Love You

Words and Music by Stevie Wonder

recorded by Stevie Wonder

No New Year's Day
To celebrate;
No chocolate-covered candy hearts
To give away.
No first of spring;
No song to sing.
In fact here's just another ordinary day.

No April rain;
No flowers bloom;
No wedding Saturday within
The month of June.
But what it is
Is something true,
Made up of these three words
I must say to you.

Refrain:
I just called to say I love you.
I just called to say how much I care.
I just called to say I love you.
And I mean it from the bottom of my heart.

No summer's high;
No warm July;
No harvest moon to light
One tender August night.
No autumn breeze;
No falling leaves;
Not even time for birds to fly
To southern skies.

No Libra sun;
No Halloween;
No giving thanks to all
The Christmas joy you bring.
But what it is,
Though old so new
To fill your heart like no
Three words could ever do.

Refrain Twice

I Say a Little Prayer

Lyric by Hal David
Music by Burt Bacharach

featured in the TriStar Motion Picture *My Best Friend's Wedding*
recorded by Dionne Warwick, Aretha Franklin

The moment I wake up
Before I put on my make-up
I say a little prayer for you.
While combing my hair now
And wondering what dress to wear now
I say a little prayer for you.

Refrain:
Forever, forever you'll stay in my heart
And I will love you forever and ever.
We never will part.
Oh, how I'll love you.
Together, together, that's how it must be
To live without you
Would only mean heartbreak for me.

I run for the bus, dear,
While riding I think of us, dear.
I say a little prayer for you.
At work I just take time
And all through my coffee break time
I say a little prayer for you.

Refrain

My darling, believe me,
For me there is no one but you.
Please love me too.
I'm in love with you
Answer my prayer.
Say you love me too.

I Swear

Words and Music by Frank Myers and Gary Baker

Recorded by All-4-One, John Michael Montgomery

I see the questions in your eyes;
I know what's weighing on your mind.
But you can be sure I know my part,
'Cause I'll stand beside you through the years;
You'll only cry those happy tears.
And though I'll make mistakes,
I'll never break your heart.

Refrain:
I swear by the moon and the stars in the sky, I'll be there.
I swear, like a shadow that's by your side, I'll be there.
For better or worse, till death do us part,
I'll love you with every beat of my heart, I swear.

I'll give you ev'rything I can;
I'll build your dreams with these two hands,
And we'll hang some mem'ries on the wall.
And when there's silver in your hair,
Won't have to ask if I still care,
'Cause as the time turns the page,
My love won't age at all.

Refrain Twice

I swear.

I Think I Love You

Words and Music by Tony Romeo

featured in the Television Series *The Partridge Family*
recorded by The Partridge Family

Bah bah bah bah…

I'm sleeping
And right in the middle of a good dream
I call out once I wake up
From something that keeps knocking
    in my brain.
Before I go insane I hold my pillow
    to my head
And spring up in my bed screaming
    out the words I dread.
I think I love you. I think I love you.

This morning
I woke up with this feeling
I didn't know how to deal with.
And so I just decided to myself I'd hide
    it to myself
And never talk about it, and did not go
    and shout it
When you walked into the room.
    I think I love you.

(I think I love you.)
I think I love you.
    So what am I so afraid of?
I'm afraid that I'm not sure of a love
    there is no cure for.
I think I love you.
    Isn't that what life is made of?
Though it worries me to say that
    I'd never felt this way.

I don't know what I'm up against.
I don't know what it's all about.
I got so much to think about.
Hey, I think I love you.
So what am I so afraid of?
I'm afraid that I'm not sure of a love
    there is no cure for.

I think I love you. Isn't that what
    life is made of?
So it worries me to say I never felt this way.
Believe me you really don't have to worry.
I only wanna make you happy
And if you say hey go away I will.
But I think better still I better stay
    around and love you.
Do you think I have a case?
Let me ask you to your face,
Do you think you love me?
Oh, I think I love you.

© 1970 (Renewed 1998) SCREEN GEMS-EMI MUSIC INC.

I Want to Spend My Lifetime Loving You

Music by James Horner
Lyric by Will Jennings

from the TriStar Motion Picture *The Mask of Zorro*
recorded by Marc Anthony & Tina Arena

Male:
Moon so bright,
Night so fine,
Keep your heart here with mine.
Life's a dream we are dreaming.

Female:
Race the moon,
Catch the wind,
Ride the night to the end.
Seize the day, stand up for the light.

Refrain:
Both:
I want to spend my lifetime loving you
If that is all in life I ever do.
Male:
Heroes rise, heroes fall.
Rise again, win it all.
Female:
In your heart, can't you feel the glory?
Through our joy, through our pain,
Both:
We can move worlds again.
Take my hand, dance with me.
Male:
Dance with me.

Both:
I want to spend my lifetime loving you
If that is all in life I ever do.
I will want nothing else to see me through
If I can spend my lifetime loving you.

Male:
Though we know we will never come again,
Where there is love,

Both:
Life begins over and over again.
Save the night, save the day.
Save the love come what may.
Love is worth everything we pay.

I want to spend my lifetime loving you
If that is all in life I ever do.
I want to spend my lifetime loving you.
If that is all in life I ever do.
I will want nothing else to see me through
If I can spend my lifetime loving you.

I Will

Words and Music by John Lennon and Paul McCartney

recorded by The Beatles

Who knows how long I've loved you,
You know I love you still.
Will I wait a lonely lifetime,
If you want me to I will.

For if I ever saw you,
I didn't catch your name.
But it never really mattered,
I will always feel the same.

Love you forever and forever,
Love you with all my heart.
Love you when we're together,
Love you when we're apart.

And when at last I find you,
Your song will fill the air.
Sing it loud so I can hear you,
For the things you do
Endear you to me.
You know I will,
I will.

I Will Be Here

Words and Music by Steven Curtis Chapman

recorded by Steven Curtis Chapman

Tomorrow mornin' if you wake up
And the sun does not appear,
I, I will be here
If in the dark we lose sight of love,
Hold my hand and have no fear
'Cause I, I will be here.

I will be here
When you feel like bein' quiet.
When you need to speak your mind,
I will listen, and I will be here.
When the laughter turns to cryin'
Through the winnin', losin' and tryin',
We'll be together,
'Cause I will be here.

Tomorrow mornin' if you wake up
And the future is unclear,
I, I will be here.
As sure as seasons are made for change,
Our lifetimes are made for years,
So I, I will be here.

I will be here,
And you can cry on my shoulder.
When the mirror tells us we're older,
I will hold you.
And I will be here
To watch you grow in beauty
And tell you all the things you are to me.
I will be here.

I will be true
To the promise I have made
To you and to the One
Who gave you to me.

I, I will be here.
And just as sure
As seasons are made for change,
Our lifetimes are made for years.

So I,
I will be here.
We'll be together.
I will be here.

I'll Be

Words and Music by Edwin McCain

recorded by Edwin McCain

The strands in your eyes
That color them wonderful
Stop me and steal my breath.
And emeralds from mountains
Thrust toward the sky,
Never revealing their depth.

Refrain 1:
And tell me that we belong together.
Dress it up with the trappings of love.
I'll be captivated,
I'll hang from your lips
Instead of the gallows of heartache
That hang from above.

Refrain 2:
I'll be your cryin' shoulder,
I'll be love suicide.
And I'll be better when I'm older,
I'll be the greatest fan of your life.

And rain falls angry on the tin roof
As we lie awake in my bed.
And you're my survival,
You're my living proof
My love is alive and not dead.

Refrain 1

Refrain 2

And I've dropped out, I've burned up.
I fought my way back from the dead.
I've tuned in, turned on, remembered the
  thing that you said.

Refrain 2 Twice

I'll Be Seeing You

Lyric by Irving Kahal
Music by Sammy Fain

from the musical *Right This Way*
a standard recorded by Frank Sinatra, Liberace and various other artists

Cathedral bells were tolling
And our hearts sang on,
Was it the spell of Paris
Or the April dawn?
Who knows
If we shall meet again?
But when the morning chimes ring sweet again:

I'll be seeing you
In all the old familiar places
That this heart of mine embraces all day through:
In that small café,
The park across the way,
The children's carrousel,
The chestnut trees, the wishing well.

I'll be seeing you
In every lovely summer's day,
In everything that's light and gay,
I'll always think of you that way.
I'll find you in the morning sun;
And when the night is new,
I'll be looking at the moon
But I'll be seeing you!

I'll Be There

Words and Music by Berry Gordy, Hal Davis, Willie Hutch and Bob West

recorded by The Jackson 5, Mariah Carey

You and I must make a pact.
We must bring salvation back.
Where there is love,
I'll be there.
(I'll be there.)
I'll reach out my hand to you,
I'll have faith in all you do.

Refrain:
Just call my name
And I'll be there.
(I'll be there.)
I'll be there to comfort you,
Build my world of dreams around you.
I'm so glad I found you.
I'll be there with a love so strong.
I'll be your strength,
You know I'll keep holding on.

Let me fill your heart with joy and laughter.
Togetherness, well it's all I'm after.
Just call my name
And I'll be there.
(I'll be there.)

I'll be there to protect you
With an unselfish love that respects you.

Refrain

If you should ever find someone new,
I know she'd better be good to you,
'Cause if she doesn't,
Then I'll be there (I'll be there.)
Don't you know, baby.
I'll be there, I'll be there.
Just call my name and I'll be there.
I'll be there, I'll be there.
Just call my name and I'll be there.

I'll Get By (As Long as I Have You)

Lyric by Roy Turk
Music by Fred E. Ahlert

a standard recorded by Dinah Shore and various other artists

This old world was just as sad a place for me
As could be,
I was lonely and blue.
This old world then changed to paradise for me
Suddenly.
Why? Because I met you.
Although wealth and power I may never find,
Still as long as I have you, dear, I won't mind.

Refrain:
For I'll get by
As long as I have you.
Though there be rain
And darkness too,
I'll not complain,
I'll laugh it through.
Poverty may come to me
That's true.
But what care I?
Say, I'll get by
As long as I have you.

Since we met my life is full of happiness,
And I guess,
It will always be so.
Just as long as I can feel your fond caress,
I'll confess,
Cares and sorrows must go.
You have turned each frown of mine into a smile.
It's your love alone that guides me all the while.

Refrain

I'll Take Romance

Lyrics by Oscar Hammerstein II
Music by Ben Oakland

from the film *I'll Take Romance*

I'll take romance,
While my heart is young and eager to fly,
I'll give my heart a try,
I'll take romance.

I'll take romance,
While my arms are strong and eager for you,
I'll give my arms their cue,
I'll take romance.

So my lover when you want me,
Call me in the hush of the evening,
When you call me,
In the hush of the evening,
I'll rush to my first real romance,
While my heart is young and eager and gay,
I'll give my heart away,
I'll take romance,
I'll take my own romance.

I'm Beginning to See the Light

Words and Music by Don George, Johnny Hodges, Duke Ellington and Harry James

a standard recorded by Duke Ellington, Harry James,
Ella Fitzgerald and various other artists

I never cared much for moon-lit skies,
I never wink back at the fire-flies.
But now that the stars are in your eyes,
I'm beginning to see the light.

I never went in for after glow,
Or candlelight on the mistletoe.
But now when you turn the lamp down low
I'm beginning to see the light.

Used to ramble through the park,
Shadow boxing in the dark.
Then you came and caused a spark,
That's a four alarm fire now.

I never made love by lantern shine,
I never saw rainbows in my wine.
But now that your lips are burning mine,
I'm beginning to see the light.

I'm Glad There Is You
(In This World of Ordinary People)

Words and Music by Paul Madeira and Jimmy Dorsey

a standard recorded by Jimmy Dorsey, Dennis Day and various other artists

In this world of ordinary people, extraordinary people,
I'm glad there is you.
In this world of overrated pleasures, of underrated treasures,
I'm glad there is you.

I'll live to love,
I'll love to be with you beside me.
This role so new, I'll muddle through with you to guide me.
In this world where many, many people play at love,
And hardly any stay in love,
I'm glad there is you.
More than ever,
I'm glad there is you.

I've Got My Love to Keep Me Warm

Words and Music by Irving Berlin

from the 20th Century Fox Motion Picture *On the Avenue*
a standard recorded by Benny Goodman and various other artists

The snow is snowing,
The wind is blowing,
But I can weather the storm.
What do I care how much it may storm?
I've got my love to keep me warm.

I can't remember
A worse December;
Just watch those icicles form.
What do I care if icicles form?
I've got my love to keep me warm.

Off with my overcoat,
Off with my glove.
I need no overcoat,
I'm burning with love.

My heart's on fire,
The flame grows higher.
So I will weather the storm.
What do I care how much it may storm?
I've got my love to keep me warm.

I've Got the World on a String

Lyric by Ted Koehler
Music by Harold Arlen

from the revue *Cotton Club Parade*
a standard recorded by Bing Crosby, Frank Sinatra and various other artists

I've got the world on a string,
Sittin' on a rainbow,
Got the string around my finger,
What a world,
What a life,
I'm in love!

I've got a song that I sing,
I cannot make the rain go,
Anytime I move my finger,
Lucky me,
Can't you see,
I'm in love?

Life is a beautiful thing,
As long as I hold the string,
I'd be a silly so and so,
If I should ever let go.
I've got the world on a string,
Sittin' on a rainbow,
Got the string around my finger,
What a world, what a life, I'm in love.

I've Got You Under My Skin

Words and Music by Cole Porter

from the film *Born to Dance*
a standard recorded by Frank Sinatra and various other artists

I've got you
Under my skin,
I've got you
Deep in the heart of me,
So deep in my heart,
You're really a part of me.
I've got you
Under my skin,
I tried so
Not to give in.
I said to myself,
"This affair never will go so well."
But why should I try to resist when, darling,
I know so well?
I've got you
Under my skin.

I'd sacrifice anything,
Come what might,
For the sake of having you near,
In spite of a warning voice
That comes in the night
And repeats and repeats in my ear:
"Don't you know, little fool,
You never can win?
Use your mentality,
Wake up to reality."
But each time I do,
Just the thought of you
Makes me stop before I begin,
'Cause I've got you
Under my skin.

If

Words and Music by David Gates

recorded by Bread

If a picture paints a thousand words,
Then why can't I paint you?
The words will never show
The you I've come to know.
If a face could launch a thousand ships,
Then where am I to go?
There's no one home but you,
You're all that's left me to.
And when my love for life is running dry,
You come and pour yourself on me.

If a man could be two places at one time,
I'd be with you;
Tomorrow and today,
Beside you all the way.
If the world should stop revolving,
Spinning slowly down to die,
I'd spend the end with you.
And when the world was through,
Then one by one, the stars would all go out.
Then you and I would simply fly away.

If Ever I Would Leave You

Words by Alan Jay Lerner
Music by Frederick Loewe

from the musical *Camelot*

If ever I would leave you
It wouldn't be in summer.
Seeing you in summer
I never would go.
Your hair streaked with sunlight,
Your lips red as flame,
Your face with a luster
That puts gold to shame!

But if I'd ever leave you,
It couldn't be in autumn,
How I'd leave in autumn
I never will know.
I've seen how you sparkle
When fall nips the air.
I know you in autumn
And I must be there.

And could I leave you running merrily through the snow?
Or on a wintry evening when you catch the fire's glow?

If ever I would leave you,
How could it be in springtime,
Knowing how in spring I'm bewitched by you so?
Oh, no! Not in springtime,
Summer, winter or fall!
No, never could I leave you at all.

If We Only Have Love (Quand on n'a que l'amour)

French Words and Music by Jacques Brel
English Words by Mort Shuman and Eric Blau

from the musical *Jacques Brel Is Alive and Well and Living in Paris*

If we only have love, then tomorrow will dawn;
And the days of our years will rise on that morn.
If we only have love, to embrace without fears;
We will kiss with our eyes, we will sleep without tears.
If we only have love, with our arms opened wide;
Then the young and the old will stand at our side.
If we only have love, love that's falling like rain;
Then the parched desert earth will grow green again.
If we only have love, for the hymn that we shout;
For the song that we sing, then we'll have a way out.

Then with nothing at all, but the little we are
We'll have conquered all time, all space, and the stars.

If we only have love, we can reach those in pain;
We can heal all our wounds, we can use our own names.
If we only have love, we can melt all the guns;
And then give the new world to our daughters and sons.
If we only have love, then Jerusalem stands;
And then death has no shadow, there are no foreign lands.
If we only have love, we will never bow down;
We'll be tall as the pines, neither heroes nor clowns.
If we only have love, then we'll only be men;
And we'll drink from the Grail, to be born once again.

Then with nothing at all, but the little we are
We'll have conquered all time, all space, and the stars.

In the Chapel in the Moonlight

Words and Music by Billy Hill

There's a little old church that's covered with moss
Where I held your hand tenderly.
I often go there to gaze at the cross
And dream that you'll come back to me.

Refrain:
How I'd love to hear the organ
In the chapel in the moonlight.
While we're strolling down the aisle where roses entwine.
How I'd love to hear you whisper
In the chapel in the moonlight
That the lovelight in your eyes forever will shine
Till the roses turn to ashes,
Till the organ turns to rust.
If you never come, I'll still be there
Till the moonlight turns to dust.
How I'd love to hear the choir
In the chapel in the moonlight
As they sing "Oh! Promise Me,"
Forever be mine.

Repeat Refrain

In the Still of the Night

Words and Music by Cole Porter

from the film *Rosalie*
a standard recorded by Frank Sinatra and various other artists

In the still of the night,
As I gaze from my window,
At the moon in its flight,
My thoughts all stray to you.

In the still of the night,
While the world is in slumber,
Oh, the times without number,
Darling, when I say to you:

Do you love me
As I love you?
Are you my life to be,
My dream come true?

Or will this dream of mine
Fade out of sight
Like the moon
Growing dim
On the rim
Of the hill
In the chill,
Still
Of the night?

In the Wee Small Hours of the Morning

Words by Bob Hilliard
Music by David Mann

recorded by Frank Sinatra and various other artists

When the sun is high in the afternoon sky,
You can always find something to do.
But from dusk till dawn as the clock ticks on,
Something happens to you.

Refrain:
In the wee small hours of the morning,
While the whole wide world is fast asleep,
You lie awake and think about the girl {boy},
And never ever think of counting sheep.
When your lonely heart has learned its lesson
You'd be hers {his} if only she {he} would call.
In the wee small hours of the morning
That's the time you miss her {him} most of all.

Repeat Refrain

Isn't It Romantic?

Words by Lorenz Hart
Music by Richard Rodgers

from the Paramount Picture *Love Me Tonight*

Verse:
I've never met you,
Yet never doubt, dear,
I can't forget you
I've thought you out, dear.
I know your profile and I know
     the way you kiss:
Just the thing I miss
On a night like this.

If dreams are made of
Imagination,
I'm not afraid of
My own creation.
With all my heart,
My heart is here for you to take.
Why should I quake?
I'm not awake.

Refrain:
Isn't it romantic?
Music in the night
A dream that can be heard.
Isn't it romantic?
Moving shadows write
The oldest magic word.

I hear the breezes playing
In the trees above,
While all the world is saying,
"You were meant for love."

Isn't it romantic?
Merely to be young
On such a night as this.
Isn't it romantic.
Every note that's sung
Is like a lover's kiss.

Sweet symbols in the moonlight,
Do you mean that I will fall
In love, perchance?
Isn't it romance?

Verse 2 (from the film): *
My face is glowing,
I'm energetic,
The art of sewing,
I found poetic.
My needle punctuates the
     rhythm of romance!
I don't give a stitch
If I don't get rich.

A custom tailor
Who has no custom,
Is like a sailor,
No one will trust 'em.
But there is magic in the music of my shears;
I shed no tears.
Lend me your ears!

In the film, the song is passed from character to character.

Refrain 2 (from the film):
Isn't it romantic?
Soon I will have found
Some girl that I adore.
Isn't it romantic?
While I sit around,
My love can scrub the floor.

She'll kiss me every hour,
Or she'll get the sack.
And when I take a shower
She can scrub my back.

Isn't it romantic?
On a moon-lit night
She'll cook me onion soup.
Kiddies are romantic
And if we don't fight,
We soon will have a troupe!

We'll help the population,
It's a duty that we owe
To dear old France.
Isn't it romance?

It Could Happen to You

Words by Johnny Burke
Music by James Van Heusen

from the Paramount Picture *And the Angels Sing*
a standard recorded by Jo Stafford, Bing Crosby and various other artists

Do you believe in charms and spells,
In mystic words and magic wands
And wishing wells?
Don't look so wise,
Don't show your scorn;
Watch yourself,
I warn you.

Hide your heart from sight,
Lock your dreams at night.
It could happen to you.
Don't count stars or you might stumble,
Someone drops a sigh,
And down you tumble.

Keep an eye on spring,
Run when church bells ring.
It could happen to you.
All I did was wonder how your arms would be
And it happened to me!

It's Been a Long, Long Time

Lyric by Sammy Cahn
Music by Jule Styne

a standard recorded by various artists

Just kiss me once, then kiss me twice,
Then kiss me once again,
It's been a long, long time.
Haven't felt like this, my dear,
Since can't remember when,
It's been a long, long time.
You'll never know how many dreams I dreamed about you,
Or just how empty they all seemed without you.
So, kiss me once, then kiss me twice,
Then kiss me once again,
It's been a long, long time.

It's Impossible (Somos novios)

English Lyric by Sid Wayne
Spanish Words and Music by Armando Manzanero

recorded by Perry Como and various other artists

It's impossible,
Tell the sun to leave the sky.
It's just impossible.
It's impossible.
Ask a baby not to cry,
It's just impossible.
Can I hold you closer to me
And not feel you going through me?
Split the second that I never think of you?
Oh how impossible.

Can the ocean keep from rushing to the shore?
It's just impossible.
If I had you
Could I ever want for more?
It's just impossible.
And tomorrow, should you
Ask me for the world
Somehow I'd get it.
I would sell my very soul and not regret it.
For to live without your love
Is just impossible,
Impossible,
Impossible.

It's Magic

Words by Sammy Cahn
Music by Jule Styne

a standard recorded by various artists

You sigh, the song begins,
You speak and I hear violins, it's magic.
The stars desert the skies
And rush to nestle in your eyes, it's magic.
Without a golden wand or mystic charms,
Fantastic things begin when I am in your arms.
When we walk hand in hand,
The world becomes a wonderland, it's magic.

How else can I explain those rainbows
When there is no rain, it's magic.
Why do I tell myself
These things that happen are all really true,
When in my heart I know
The magic is my love for you.

It's Your Love

Words and Music by Stephony E. Smith

recorded by Tim McGraw with Faith Hill

Male:
Dancin' in the dark,
Middle of the night.
Takin' your heart
And holdin' it tight.
Emotional touch
Touchin' my skin,
And askin' you to do
What you've been doin' all over again.

Refrain:
Oh, it's a beautiful thing
Don't think I can keep it all in.
I just gotta let you know
What it is that won't let me go.
Both:
It's your love.
It just does somethin' to me
It sends a shock right through me.
I can't get enough.
And if you wonder
About the spell I'm under,
It's your love.
Male:
Better than I was,
More than I am,
And all of this happened
By takin' your hand.
And who I am now
Is who I wanted to be.

Both:
And now that we're together,
I'm stronger than ever.
I'm happy and free.
Oh, it's a beautiful thing,
Don't think I can keep it all in.
Male:
Oh, did you ask me why I've changed?
All I gotta do is say your sweet name.
Both:
It's your love.
It just does something' to me.
It sends a shock right through me.
I can't get enough.
And if you wonder
About the spell I'm under,
It's your love.

It's a beautiful thing.

June in January

Words and Music by Leo Robin and Ralph Rainger

from the Paramount Picture *Here Is My Heart*
a standard recorded by various artists

It's June in January because I'm in love;
It always is spring in my heart with you in my arms.
The snow is just white blossoms that fall from above.
And here is the reason, my dear, your magical charms.

The night is cold, the trees are bare,
But I can feel the scent of roses in the air.
It's June in January because I'm in love,
But only because I'm in love with you.

Just the Way You Are

Words and Music by Billy Joel

recorded by Billy Joel

Don't go changing to try and please me,
You never let me down before.
Don't imagine you're too familiar,
And I don't see you anymore.

I would not leave you in times of trouble,
We never could have come this far.
I took the good times,
    I'll take the bad times,
I'll take you just the way you are.

Don't go trying some new fashion,
Don't change the color of your hair.
You always have my unspoken passion,
Although I might not seem to care.

I don't want clever conversation,
I never want to work that hard.
I just want someone that I can talk to,
I want you just the way you are.

I need to know that you will always be
The same old someone that I knew.
Oh, what will it take till you believe in me,
The way that I believe in you.

I said I love you and that's forever,
And this I promise from the heart.
I could not love you any better,
I love you just the way you are.

I don't want clever conversation,
I never want to work that hard.
I just want someone that I can talk to,
I want you just the way you are.

The Keeper of the Stars

Words and Music by Karen Staley, Danny Mayo and Dickey Lee

recorded by Tracy Byrd

It was no accident, me finding you.
Someone had a hand in it long before we ever knew.
Now I just can't believe you're in my life.
Heaven's smiling down on me as I look at you tonight.

I tip my hat to the keeper of the stars.
He sure knew what he was doin'
When he joined these two hearts.
I hold everything when I hold you in my arms.
I've got all I'll ever need, thanks to the keeper of the stars.

Soft moonlight on your face, oh, how you shine.
It takes my breath away just to look into your eyes.
I know I don't deserve a treasure like you.
There really are no words to show my gratitude.

So I tip my hat to the keeper of the stars.
He sure knew what he was doin'
When he joined these two hearts.
I hold everything when I hold you in my arms.
I've got all I'll ever need, thanks to the keeper of the stars.

It was no accident, me finding you.
Someone had a hand in it long before we ever knew.

L-O-V-E

Words and Music by Bert Kaempfert and Milt Gabler

recorded by Nat "King" Cole and various other artists

L is for the way you look at me.
O is for the only one I see.
V is very, very extraordinary.
E is even more than anyone that you adore can.

Love is all that I can give to you,
Love is more than just a game for two.
Two in love can make it.
Take my heart and please don't break it,
Love was made for me and you.

Repeat Song

(That's almost true)
For me and you.

Lady in Red

Words and Music by Chris DeBurgh

recorded by Chris DeBurgh

I've never seen you looking so lovely as you did tonight;
I've never seen you shine so bright.
I've never seen so many men ask you if you wanted to dance.
They're looking for a little romance,
Given half a chance.
I have never seen that dress you're wearing,
Or the highlights in your hair that catch your eyes.
I have been blind.

Refrain:
The lady in red is dancing with me,
Cheek to cheek.
There's nobody here, it's just you and me.
It's where I wanna be.
But I hardly know this beauty by my side.
I'll never forget the way you look tonight.

I've never seen you looking so gorgeous as you did tonight;
I've never seen you shine so bright.
You were amazing.
I've never seen so many people
Want to be there by your side,
And when you turned to me and smiled,
It took my breath away.
I have never had such a feeling,
Such a feeling of complete and utter love
As I do tonight.

Refrain

I never will forget the way you look tonight.
The lady in red. The lady in red. The lady in red.
My lady in red.
Spoken: I love you.

Let It Rain

Words and Music by Eric Clapton and Bonnie Bramlett

recorded by Eric Clapton

The rain is falling
Through the mist of sorrow that surrounded me.
The sun could melt the fog away,
The mist that may surround me.

Refrain:
Let it rain; let it rain.
Let your love rain down on me.
Let it rain; let it rain.
Let it rain, rain, rain.

My life was like a desert flower,
Burning in the sun.
Until I found the way to love,
The heart was sad and done.

Refrain

Now I know the secret;
There is nothing that I lack.
If I give my love to you,
Be sure to give it back.

Refrain

Let There Be Love

Lyric by Ian Grant
Music by Lionel Rand

a standard recorded by Sammy Kaye, Pearl Bailey and various other artists

Let there be you
And let there be me,
Let there be oysters
Under the sea.

Let there be wind
An occasional rain,
Chile con carne
And sparkling champagne.

Let there be birds
To sing in the trees,
Someone to bless me
Whenever I sneeze.

Let there be cuckoos,
A lark and a dove
But first of all,
Please let there be love.

Let's Stay Together

Words and Music by Al Green, Willie Mitchell and Al Jackson, Jr.

recorded by Al Green

I'm, I'm so in love with you.
Whatever you want to do is alright with me.
'Cause you make me feel so brand new,
And now I want to spend my life with you.

Let me say since, baby, since we've been together,
Lovin' you forever is what I need.
Let me be the one you come running to,
And I'll never be untrue.

Oh, baby, let's stay together,
Loving you whether times are good or bad,
Happy or sad.
Baby times are good or bad, happy or sad.

Why, why people break up
Turn around and make up I just can't see.
You'd never do that to me,
Being around you is all I see.

It's why I beg you, let's stay together,
Loving you whether times are good or bad,

Repeat and Fade:
Babe, let's stay together.

Longer

Words and Music by Dan Fogelberg

recorded by Dan Fogelberg

Longer than there've been fishes in the ocean,
Higher than any bird ever flew,
Longer than there've been stars up in the heavens,
I've been in love with you.

Stronger than any mountain cathedral,
Truer than any tree ever grew,
Deeper than any forest primeval,
I am in love with you.

I'll bring
Fires in the winters;
You'll send
Showers in the springs.
We'll fly
Through the falls and summers
With love on our wings.

Through the years as the fire starts to mellow,
Burning lines in the book of our lives.
Though the binding cracks and pages start to yellow,
I'll be in love with you.
I'll be in love with you

Repeat Verse 1

I am in love with you.

The Look of Love

Words by Hal David
Music by Burt Bacharach

from the film *Casino Royale*
recorded by Sergio Mendes & Brasil '66

The look of love is in your eyes,
A look your smile can't disguise.
The look of love, it's saying so
Much more than just words could ever say
And what my heart has heard,
Well, it takes my breath away.
I can hardly wait to hold you,
Feel my arms around you,
How long I have waited,
Waited just to love you,
Now that I have found you

You've got the look of love
It's on your face,
A look that time can't erase.
Be mine tonight, let this be just
The start of so many nights like this
Let's take a lover's vow
And then seal it with a kiss.
I can hardly wait to hold you,
Feel my arms around you,
How long I have waited,
Waited just to love you,
Now that I have found you
Don't ever go,
Don't ever go,
I love you so.

Love Is a Simple Thing

Words by June Carroll
Music by Arthur Siegel

a standard recorded by various artists

Love is a simple thing,
Love is a silver ring,
Shiny as a ribbon bow,
Soft as a quiet snow.
Love is a nursery rhyme,
Old as the tick of time.
Love is so many things,
Bright as an angel's wings,
Gentle as the morning light,
Long as a winter night.
Love makes an old heart sing
And it fills ev'ry empty space;
Love is a warming place,
Love is a simple thing.

Love is a simple thing,
Love is a magic ring,
Much more fun than mistletoe,
Gay as a puppet show.
Love is the thunder and rain,
Swift as a soaring plane.
Love is a summer moon,
Gay as a big balloon,
Wild as a storm at sea,
Young as a calliope.
Love is a touch of spring,
It's as sweet as a first embrace,
Love is a special face,
Love is a simple thing.

Love Is Just Around the Corner

Words and Music by Leo Robin and Lewis E. Gensler

from the Paramount Picture *Here Is My Heart*

Love is just around the corner, any cozy little corner,
Love is just around the corner, when I'm around you.
I'm a sentimental mourner, and I couldn't be more forlorner.
When you keep me on a corner just waiting for you.

Venus de Milo was not noted for her charms.
But strictly between us, you're cuter than Venus
And what's more you've got arms.
So let's go cuddle in a corner, any cozy little corner,
Love is just around the corner, and I'm around you.

Love Is the Sweetest Thing

Words and Music by Ray Noble

a standard recorded by various artists

Whether you're twenty and starting in life;
Whether to thirty you've grown;
Whether to forty a husband or wife;
Whether you're fifty, a Darby or Joan;
There's one thing certain that you'll have to own:

Refrain:
Love is the sweetest thing,
What else on earth could ever bring
Such happiness to ev'rything
As love's old story.
Love is the strangest thing,
No song of birds upon the wing
Shall in our hearts more sweetly sing
Than love's old story.
Whatever heart may desire,
Whatever fate may send,
This is the tale that never will tire.
This is the song without end.
Love is the greatest thing,
The oldest yet the latest thing,
I only hope that fate can bring
Love's story to you.

Whether you've gone after worldly success,
Making your place in the sun;
Whether your income's one million or less,
Just when you think all the prizes you've won,
You'll wake to learn after all's said and done:

Refrain

Love Letters

Words by Edward Heyman
Music by Victor Young

Theme from the Paramount Picture *Love Letters*
Recorded by Ketty Lester, Elvis Presley and various other artists

The sky may be starless, the night may be moonless,
But deep in my heart there's a glow,
For deep in my heart I know that you love me.
You love me because you told me so!

Love letters straight from your heart
Keep us so near while apart.
I'm not alone in the night
When I can have all the love you write.
I memorize ev'ry line,
I kiss the name that you sign,
And darling, then I read again right from the start,
Love letters straight from your heart.

Love Me Tender

Words and Music by Elvis Presley and Vera Matson

from the film *Love Me Tender*
recorded by Elvis Presley

Love me tender, love me sweet;
Never let me go.
You have made me life complete,
And I love you so.

Refrain:
Love me tender, love me true
All my dreams fulfill.
For, my darlin', I love you,
And I always will.

Love me tender, love me long;
Take me to your heart.
For it's there that I belong,
And we'll never part.

Refrain

Love me tender, love me dear;
Tell me you are mine.
I'll be yours through all the years,
Till the end of time.

Refrain

Love Me with All Your Heart
(Cuendo calienta el sol)

Original Words and Music by Carlos Rigual and Carlos A. Martinoli
English Words by Sunny Skylar

recorded by The Ray Charles Singers, The Bachelors and various other artists

Love me with all your heart,
That's all I want, love.
Love me with all of your heart or not at all.

Just promise me this:
That you'll give me all your kisses,
Every winter, every summer, every fall.

When we are far apart
Or when you are near me,
Love me with all of your heart as I love you.
Don't give me your love for a moment or an hour,
Love me always as you loved me from the start,
With every beat of your heart.

Love of a Lifetime

Words and Music by Bill Leverty and Carl Snare

recorded by Firehouse

I guess the time was right for us to say
We'd take our time and live our lives together day by day.
We'll make a wish and send it on a prayer.
We know our dreams can all come true,
With love that we can share.

With you I never wonder,
"Will you be there for me?"
With you I never wonder.
You're the right one for me.

Refrain:
I finally found the love of a lifetime,
A love to last my whole life through.
I finally found the love of a lifetime forever in my heart.
I finally found the love of a lifetime.

With every kiss, our love is like brand new
And every star up in the sky was made for me and you.
Still, we both know that the road is long,
But we know that we will be together
Because our love is strong.

Refrain Twice

I finally found the love of a lifetime...

Love of My Life

Words and Music by Jim Brickman and Tom Douglas

recorded by Jim Brickman with Michael W. Smith

I am amazed.
When I look at you,
I see you smiling back at me.
It's like all my dreams come true.

I am afraid.
If I lost you girl,
I'd fall through the cracks
   and lose my track
In this crazy, lonely world.

Sometimes it's so hard to believe,
When the nights can be so long,
And faith gave me the strength
And kept me holding on.

Refrain:
You are the love of my life,
And I'm so glad you found me.
You are the love of my life.
Baby, put your arms around me.
I guess this is how it feels
When you finally find something real.
My angel in the night,
You are my love
The love of my life.

Now here you are,
With midnight closing in.
You take my hand as our shadows dance,
With moonlight on your skin.

I look in your eyes.
I'm lost inside your kiss.
I think if I'd never met you
About all the things I'd missed.

Sometimes it's so hard to believe
When a love can be so strong
And faith gave me the strength
And kept me holding on.

Refrain Twice

Love Will Keep Us Together

Words and Music by Neil Sedaka and Howard Greenfield

recorded by Captain & Tenille

Love will keep us together;
Think of me, babe, whenever
Some sweet-talkin' guy comes along,
Singin' his song.
Don't mess around;
You gotta be strong.

Refrain:
Just stop,
'Cause I really love ya;
Stop, I'll be thinkin' of ya.
Look in my heart and let love
Keep us together.

You, you belong to me now;
Ain't gonna set you free now.
When those guys start hangin' around,
Talkin' me down,
Hear with your heart
And you won't hear a sound.

Refrain

…Whatever.
Young and beautiful,
But someday your looks will be gone.
When others turn you off,
Who'll be turning you on?
I will, I will, I will.

I will be there to share forever;
Love will keep us together.
Said it before and I'll say it again,
While others pretend,
I need you now and I'll need you then.

Refrain

…Whatever.

Lover

Words by Lorenz Hart
Music by Richard Rodgers

from the Paramount Picture *Love Me Tonight*
a standard recorded by Ella Fitzgerald, Peggy Lee and various other artists

When you held your hand to my heart,
Dear, you did something grand to my heart,
And we played the scene to perfection,
Though we didn't have time to rehearse.
Since you took control of my life
You have become the whole of my life.
When you are away, it's awful,
And when you are with me, it's worse.

Lover, when I'm near you,
And I hear you speak my name
Softly in my ear, you breathe a flame.
Lover, when we're dancing,
Keep on glancing in my eyes
Till love's own entrancing music dies.
All of my future is in you.
Your ev'ry plan I design.
Promise you'll always continue to be mine.
Lover, please be tender.
When you're tender, fears depart.
Lover, I surrender to my heart.

Lover, when I'm near you,
And I hear you speak my name
Softly in my ear, you breathe a flame.
Lover, it's immoral,
But why quarrel with our bliss
When two lips of coral want to kiss?
I say, "The Devil is in you,"
And to resist you I try;
But if you didn't continue, I would die!
Lover, please be tender.
When you're tender, fears depart.
Lover, I surrender to my heart.

Memories Are Made of This

Words and Music by Richard Dehr, Frank Miller and Terry Gilkyson

recorded by Dean Martin, Gale Storm

Take one fresh and tender kiss.
Add one stolen night of bliss.
One girl, one boy:
Some grief, some joy.
Memories are made of this.

Don't forget a small moonbeam.
Fold in lightly with a dream.
Your lips and mine,
Two sips of wine.
Memories are made of this.

Then add the wedding bells,
One house where lovers dwell,
Three little kids for the flavor.
Stir carefully through the days;
See how the flavor stays,
These are the dreams you will savor.

With the blessings from above,
Serve it generously with love.
One man, one love, through life,
Memories are made of this.

Makin' Whoopee!

Lyrics by Gus Kahn
Music by Walter Donaldson

from the musical *Whoopee!*
a standard recorded by various artists

Ev'rytime I hear that march
   from *Lohengrin*,
I am always on the outside looking in.
Maybe that is why I see the funny side,
When I see a fallen brother take a bride.
Weddings make a lot of people sad.
But if you're not the groom,
   they're not so bad.

Another bride,
Another June,
Another sunny
Honeymoon.
Another season,
Another reason,
For makin' whoopee!

A lot of shoes
A lot of rice,
The groom is nervous
He answers twice.
It's really killing
That he's so willing
To make whoopee!

Picture a little love-nest,
Down where the roses cling.
Picture the same sweet love-nest,
Think what a year can bring.

He's washing dishes,
And baby clothes,
He's so ambitious,
He even sews.
But don't forget folks,
That's what you get, folks,
For makin' whoopee!

Another year,
Or maybe less.
What's this I hear?
Well, can't you guess?
She feels neglected,
And he's suspected,
Of makin' whoopee!

She sits alone,
'Most ev'ry night.
He doesn't phone her,
He doesn't write.
He says he's "busy"
But she says "is he?"
He's makin' whoopee!

He doesn't make much money,
Only five thousand per.
Some judge who thinks he's funny,
Says "you'll pay six to her."

He says, "Now judge,
Suppose I fail?"
The judge says, "Budge
Right into jail."
You'd better keep her,
I think it's cheaper,
Than makin' whoopee!

Misty

Words by Johnny Burke
Music by Erroll Garner

a standard recorded by Johnny Mathis and various other artists

Look at me,
I'm as helpless as a kitten up a tree,
And I feel like I'm clinging to a cloud,
I can't understand,
I get misty just holding your hand.

Walk my way,
And a thousand violins begin to play,
Or it might be the sound of your hello,
That music I hear,
I get misty, the moment you're near.

You can say that you're leading me on,
But it's just what I want you to do,
Don't you notice how hopelessly I'm lost,
That's why I'm following you.

On my own,
Would I wander through this wonderland alone,
Never knowing my right foot from my left,
My hat from my glove,
I'm too misty and too much in love.

A Month of Sundays

Words by Johnny Mercer
Music by Robert Emmett Dolan

a standard recorded by various artists

First date I had with you I kissed you.
Do you recall what I said then?
One way to tell me how I've missed you
Would be to say it once again.

Refrain:
I'm glad I waited a month of Sundays
To find somebody like you.
I've seen more daybreaks turn into lonely nights.
Those signs on Broadway should have that many lights.
Have you tried waiting a month of Sundays
For just one dream come true?
I'll have to own up, that if you hadn't shown up,
There'd only be one thing to do,
I'd wait a million months of Sundays for you.

Repeat Refrain

Moonglow

Words and Music by Will Hudson, Eddie De Lange and Irving Mills

a standard recorded by Morris Stoloff, George Cates and various other artists

Like someone that hasn't any country,
Like a stranger visiting from Mars,
I went around alone, just like a rolling stone,
Until I read a message in the stars:

Refrain:
It must have been moonglow,
Way up in the blue.
It must have been moonglow
That led me straight to you.
I still hear you saying,
"Dear one, hold me fast."
And I start in praying,
Oh Lord, please let this last.
We seem to float right through the air.
Heavenly songs seem to come from ev'rywhere.
And now when there's moonglow,
Way up in the blue,
I always remember
That moonglow gave me you.

Repeat Refrain

Moonlight Becomes You

Words by Johnny Burke
Music by James Van Heusen

from the Paramount Picture *Road to Morocco*
a standard recorded by Glenn Miller, Harry James, Frank Sinatra and various other artists

Stand there just a moment, darling,
Let me catch my breath.
I've never seen a picture quite so lovely.
How did you ever learn to look so lovely?

Moonlight becomes you,
It goes with your hair,
You certainly know the right thing to wear.

Moonlight becomes you,
I'm thrilled at the sight.
And I could get so romantic tonight.

You're all dressed up to go dreaming,
Now don't tell me I'm wrong,
And what a night to go dreaming,
Mind if I tag along?

If I say I love you,
I want you to know
It's not just because there's moonlight,
Although moonlight becomes you.

Moonlight Cocktail

Lyric by Kim Gannon
Music by Lucky Roberts

from the film *A Night in Casablanca*
a standard recorded by Glenn Miller with Ray Eberle and various other artists

Coupl'a jiggers of moonlight and add a star.
Pour in the blue of a June night and one guitar.
Mix in a coupl'a dreamers and there you are.
Lovers hail the moonlight cocktail.

Now add a coupl'a flowers, a drop of dew,
Stir for a coupl'a hours till dreams come true.
As to the number of kisses, it's up to you.
Moonlight cocktails need a few.

Cool it in the summer breeze,
Serve it in the starlight underneath the trees.
You'll discover tricks like these
Are sure to make your moonlight cocktail please.

Follow the simple directions and they will bring
Life of another complexion, where you'll be king.
You will awake in the morning and start to sing.
Moonlight cocktails are the thing.

Moonlight in Vermont

Words and Music by John Blackburn and Karl Suessdorf

a standard recorded by various artists

Pennies in a stream,
Falling leaves, a sycamore,
Moonlight in Vermont.

Icy finger waves,
Ski trails on a mountainside,
Snowlight in Vermont.

Telegraph cables, they sing down the highway
And travel each bend in the road.
People who meet in this romantic setting
Are so hypnotized by the lovely

Evening summer breeze,
Warbling of a meadowlark,
Moonlight in Vermont.

You and I and moonlight in Vermont.

More (Ti guardero' nel cuore)

Music by Nino Oliviero and Riz Ortolani
Italian Lyrics by Marcello Ciorciolini
English Lyrics by Norman Newell

from the film *Mondo Cane*
recorded by Kai Winding, Vic Dana and various other artists

More than the greatest love the world has known;
This is the love I'll give to you alone.
More than the simple words I try to say;
I only live to love you more each day.

More than you'll ever know,
My arms long to hold you so,
My life will be in your keeping,
Walking, sleeping, laughing, weeping.

Longer than always is a long, long time,
But far beyond forever you'll be mine.
I know I never lived before,
And my heart is very sure,
No one else could love you more.

More Than Words

Words and Music by Nuno Bettencourt and Gary Cherone

recorded by Extreme

Sayin', "I love you"
Is not the words I want to hear from you.
It's not that I want you not to say.
But if you only knew how easy it would be,
To show me how you feel,
More than words is all you have to do to make it real.
Then you wouldn't have to say that you love me,
'Cause I'd already know.

Refrain:
What would you do if my heart was torn in two?
More than words to show you feel
That your love for me is real.
What would you say if I took those words away?
Then you couldn't make things new
Just by sayin', "I love you."

La di da da di da…
More than words.

Now that I have tried to talk to you
And make you understand.
All you have to do is close your eyes
And just reach out your hands.
And touch me, hold me close, don't ever let me go.

More than words is all I ever needed you to show.
Then you wouldn't have to say
That you love me,
'Cause I'd already know.

Refrain

More than words.

More Today Than Yesterday

Words and Music by Pat Upton

recorded by Spiral Starecase

I don't remember what day it was;
I didn't notice what time it was.
All I know is that I fell in love with you.
And if all my dreams come true,
I'll be spending time with you.

Ev'ry day's a new day in love with you.
With each day comes a new way of loving you.
Ev'ry time I kiss your lips my mind starts to wander.
If all my dreams come true,
I'll be spending time with you.

Refrain:
Oh, I love you more today than yesterday,
But not as much as tomorrow.
I love you more today than yesterday,
But darling, not as much as tomorrow.

Tomorrow's date means springtime's just a day away.
Cupid, we don't need you now, be on your way.
I thank the Lord for love like ours that grows ever stronger.
And I always will be true,
I know you feel the same way too.

Refrain

Ev'ry day's a new day, ev'ry time I love you.
Ev'ry way's a new way, ev'ry time I love you.

My All

Words by Mariah Carey
Music by Mariah Carey and Walter Afanasieff

recorded by Mariah Carey

I am thinking of you
In my sleepless solitude tonight.
If it's wrong to love you,
Then my heart just won't let me be right
'Cause I've drowned in you
And I won't pull through
Without you by my side.

Refrain:
I'd give my all to have
Just one more night with you.
I'd risk my life to feel
Your body next to mine,
'Cause I can't go on
Living in the memory of our song.
I'd give my all for your love tonight.

Baby, can you feel me
Imagining I'm looking in your eyes?
I can see you clearly,
Vividly emblazoned in my mind,
And yet you're so far,
Like a distant star
I'm wishing on tonight.

Refrain Twice

Give my all for your love tonight.

My Cherie Amour

Words and Music by Stevie Wonder, Sylvia Moy and Henry Cosby

recorded by Stevie Wonder

La la la la la la,
La la la la la la.

My cherie amour, lovely as a summer day,
My cherie amour, distant as the Milky Way.
My cherie amour, pretty little one that I adore,
You're the only girl my heart beats for;
How I wish that you were mine.

In a café or sometimes on a crowded street,
I've been near you, but you never noticed me.
My cherie amour, won't you tell me how could you ignore
That behind that little smile I wore,
How I wish that you were mine.

La la la la la la,
La la la la la la.

Maybe someday you'll see my face among the crowd.
Maybe someday I'll share your little distant cloud.
Oh cherie amour, pretty little one that I adore,
You're the only girl my heart beats for;
How I wish that you were mine.

La la la la la la,
La la la la la la.

My Foolish Heart

Words by Ned Washington
Music by Victor Young

from the film *My Foolish Heart*
a standard recorded by Billy Eckstine and various other artists

The night is like a lovely tune,
Beware my foolish heart!
How white the ever constant moon;
Take care my foolish heart!
There's a line between love and fascination
That's hard to see on an evening such as this,
For they both give the very same sensation
When you're lost in the magic of a kiss.

His {Her} lips are much too close to mine,
Beware my foolish heart;
But should our eager lips combine
Then let the fire start.
For this time it isn't fascination,
Or a dream that will fade and fall apart,
It's love this time, it's love, my foolish heart.

My Funny Valentine

Words by Lorenz Hart
Music by Richard Rodgers

from the musical *Babes in Arms*
a standard recorded by many various artists

Behold the way our fine-feathered friend
His virtue doth parade.
Though knowest not, my dim-witted friend,
The picture thou hast made.
Thy vacant brow and thy tousled hair
Conceal thy good intent.
Thou noble, upright, truthful, sincere,
And slightly dopey gent, you're…

My funny Valentine,
Sweet comic Valentine,
You make me smile with my heart.
Your looks are laughable,
Unphotographable,
Yet you're my favorite work of art.
Is your figure less than Greek?
Is your mouth a little weak?
When you open it to speak
Are you smart?
But don't change a hair for me,
Not if you care for me,
Stay, little Valentine, stay!
Each day is Valentine's Day.

My Heart Will Go On (Love Theme from 'Titanic')

Music by James Horner
Lyric by Will Jennings

from the Paramount and Twentieth Century Fox Motion Picture *Titanic*
recorded by Celine Dion

Every night in my dreams I see you, I feel you.
That is how I know you go on.
Far across the distance and spaces between us
You have come to show you go on.

Refrain:
Near, far, wherever you are,
I believe that the heart does go on.
Once more you open the door
And you're here in my heart,
And my heart will go on and on.

Love can touch us one time
And last for a lifetime,
And never let go till we're gone.
Love was when I loved you;
One true time I hold to.
In my life we'll always go on.

Refrain

You're here, there's nothing I fear
And I know that my heart will go on.
We'll stay forever this way.
You are safe in my heart,
And my heart will go on and on.

My Ideal

Words by Leo Robin
Music by Richard A. Whiting and Newell Chase

from the Paramount Picture *Playboy of Paris*
a standard recorded by various artists

Long ago my heart and mind
Got together and designed
The wonderful girl for me.
Oh, what a fantasy.
Though the idol of my heart
Can't be ordered à la carte
I wonder if she will be
Always a fantasy.

Will I ever find the girl in my mind,
The one who is my ideal?
Maybe she's a dream, and yet she might be
Just around the corner waiting for me.
Will I recognize a light in her eyes
That no other eyes reveal?
Or will I pass her by and never even know
That she is my ideal?

Will I ever find the girl in my mind,
The one who is my ideal?
Maybe she's a dream, and yet she might be
Just around the corner waiting for me.
Will I recognize a light in her eyes
That no other eyes reveal?
Although she may be late, I trust in fate,
And so I wait for my ideal.

My One and Only Love

Words by Robert Mellin
Music by Guy Wood

a standard recorded by various artists

The very thought of you makes my heart sing
Like an April breeze on the wings of spring,
And you appear in all your splendor,
My one and only love.

The shadows fall and spread their mystic charms
In the hush of night while you're in my arms.
I feel your lips, so warm and tender,
My one and only love.

The touch of your hand is like heaven,
A heaven that I've never known.
The blush on your cheek whenever I speak
Tells me that you are my own.

You fill my cager heart with such desire.
Ev'ry kiss you give sets my soul on fire.
I give myself in sweet surrender,
My one and only love.

My Romance

Words by Lorenz Hart
Music by Richard Rodgers

from the musical *Jumbo*
a standard recorded by Morton Downey, Margaret Whiting, Dave Brubeck,
Doris Day and various other artists

I won't kiss your hand, madam,
Crazy for you though I am.
I'll never woo you on bended knee,
No, madam, not me.
We don't need that flowery fuss.
No sir, madam, not for us.

My romance
Doesn't have to have a moon in the sky.
My romance
Doesn't need a blue lagoon standing by.
No month of May,
No twinkling stars.
No hideaway,

No soft guitars.
My romance
Doesn't need a castle rising in Spain,
Nor a dance
To a constantly surprising refrain.
Wide awake,
I can make my most fantastic dreams come true.
My romance
Doesn't need a thing but you.

My Silent Love

Words by Edward Heyman
Music by Dana Suesse

a standard recorded by various artists

You would only spurn my love if I had shown it.
You would surely turn my love away.
You and I are miles apart, I've always known it.
I just make my smiles a part of the game that I must play.

I reach for you like I'd reach for a star,
Worshipping you from afar,
Living with my silent love.
I'm like a flame dying out in the rain,
Only the ashes remain,
Smold'ring like my silent love.
How I long to tell all the things I have planned,
Still, it's wrong to tell, you would not understand.
You'll go along never dreaming I care,
Loving somebody somewhere,
Leaving me my silent love.

The Nearness of You

Words by Ned Washington
Music by Hoagy Carmichael

from the Paramount Picture *Romance in the Dark*
a standard recorded by various artists

It's not the pale moon that excites me,
That thrills and delights me.
Oh no, it's just the nearness of you.

It isn't your sweet conversation
That brings this sensation,
Oh no, it's just the nearness of you.

When you're in my arms,
And I feel you so close to me,
All my wildest dreams come true.

I need no soft light to enchant me,
If only you'll grant me
The right
To hold you ever so tight,
And to feel in the night,
The nearness of you.

Nevertheless (I'm in Love with You)

Words and Music by Bert Kalmar and Harry Ruby

a standard recorded by Frank Sinatra and various other artists

Maybe I'm right, and maybe I'm wrong,
Maybe I'm weak, and maybe I'm strong;
But nevertheless, I'm in love with you.

Maybe I'll win and maybe I'll lose,
Maybe I'm in for cryin' the blues;
But nevertheless, I'm in love with you.

Somehow I know at a glance
The terrible chances I'm taking.
Fine at the start,
Then left with a heart that is breaking.

Maybe I'll live a life of regret,
And maybe I'll give much more than I'll get;
But nevertheless, I'm in love with you.

The Next Time I Fall

Words and Music by Paul Gordon and Bobby Caldwell

recorded by Peter Cetera with Amy Grant

Love, like a road that never ends.
How it leads me back again
To heartache,
I'll never understand.
Darling, I put my heart upon the shelf
'Til the moment was right. And I tell myself

Refrain:
Next time I fall in love
I'll know better what to do.
Next time I fall in love,
Ooh, Ooh, Ooh.
The next time I fall in love,
The next time I fall in love
It will be with you.

Oh, now, as I look into your eyes,
Well, I wonder if it's wise
To hold you like I've wanted to before.

Tonight, ooh, I was thinking that you might
Be the one who breathes life in this heart of mine.

Refrain

(It will be with you.)
Next time I'm gonna follow through.
And if it drives me crazy,
I will know better why
The next time I try.

Refrain Twice

A Nightingale Sang in Berkeley Square

Lyric by Eric Maschwitz
Music by Manning Sherwin

a standard recorded by various artists

Note: Berkeley is pronounced Barkly

That certain night, the night we met,
There was magic abroad in the air.
There were angels dining at the Ritz,
And a nightingale sang in Berkeley Square.

I may be right, I may be wrong,
But I'm perfectly willing to swear
That when you turned and smiled at me
A nightingale sang in Berkeley Square.

The moon that lingered over London town,
Poor puzzled moon, he wore a frown.
How could he know we two were so in love?
The whole darn world seemed upside down.

The streets of town were paved with stars
It was such a romantic affair.
And as we kissed and said "goodnight,"
A nightingale sang in Berkeley Square.

How strange it was, how sweet and strange,
There was never a dream to compare
With that hazy, crazy night we met,
When a nightingale sang in Berkeley Square.

This heart of mine beats loud and fast,
Like a merry-go-round in a fair,
For we were dancing cheek to cheek
And a nightingale sang in Berkeley Square.

When dawn came stealing up all gold and
blue
To interrupt our rendezvous,
I still remember how you smiled and said,
"Was that a dream or was it true?"

Our homeward step was just as light
As the tap-dancing feet of Astaire
And like an echo far away,
A nightingale sang in Berkeley Square.

I know 'cause I was there,
That night in Berkeley Square.

No Two People

By Frank Loesser

from the Motion Picture *Hans Christian Andersen*

Note: The song is a duet; the male lines are in parentheses

Never before and never again
Could anything more romantic and beautiful be!
(Never before and never again,
No two people have ever been so in love.)
Been so in love, been so in love
(Been so in love, been so in love),
It's incredible no two people
Have ever been so in love as my lovey dove
(Been so as my lovey dove and I).

And this is unique, the positive peak,
Oh, we are the most unusual couple on earth.
(No two people have ever mooned such a moon)
Mooned such a moon (Juned such a June),
Juned such a June (spooned such a spoon).
What he means is that
No two people have ever been so in tune
(Been so) as my macaroon and I.

(And when we kiss, and when we kiss.)
And when we kiss, well, it's like this.
(Well, it's historical, it's hysterical.)
Let me tell it. (Well, certainly darling.)
No two people have ever been so in love
(Been so in love, been so in love),
Been so in love, been so in love.
(It's impossible no two people have ever been so in love)
Been so as my lovey dove and
(As my lovey dove and I).
And this is the cream, the very extreme,
The sort of a dream you couldn't imagine at all.
(Well, anyway, no two people have ever been so in love)
Been so as my lovey dove and I.

On a Slow Boat to China

By Frank Loesser

a standard recorded by various artists

I'd love to get you
On a slow boat to China,
All to myself alone.
Get you and keep you, in your arms evermore,
Leave all your lovelies (lovers)
Weeping on the faraway shore.

Out on the briny
With the moon big and shiny,
Melting your heart of stone.
I'd love to get you
On a slow boat to China,
All to myself alone.

There is no verse to this song,
'Cause I don't want to wait a moment too long.

On the Wings of Love

Words and Music by Jeffrey Osborne and Peter Schless

recorded by Jeffrey Osborne

Just smile for me and let the day begin.
You are the sunshine that lights my heart within.
And I'm sure that you're an angel in disguise.
Come take my hand and together we will ride.

Refrain:
On the wings of love, up and above the clouds;
The only way to fly is on the wings of love.
On the wings of love,
Only the two of us together flying high.

You look at me and I begin to melt,
Just like the snow, when a ray of sun is felt.
And I'm crazy 'bout you, baby, can't you see?
I'd be so delighted if you would come with me.

Refrain

Yes, you belong to me, and I'm yours exclusively.
And right now we live and breathe together.
Inseparable it seems, we're flowing like a stream running free.
Traveling on the wings of love.

Refrain

Together flying high.

Refrain

Flying high upon the wings of love, of love.

One Dozen Roses

Words by Roger Lewis and "Country" Joe Washburn
Music by Dick Jurgens and Walter Donovan

You say my uncle left a million,
And half of it belongs to me?
Let us talk about that later,
It's important, but love's greater,
Right now I'm busy as a bee.
I'm in an awful hurry,
So don't ask me now to stop,
I'm going to place an order
In a little flower shop.

Refrain:
Give me one dozen roses,
Put my heart in beside them,
And send them to the one I love.
She'll be glad to receive them,
And I know she'll believe them,
That's something we've been talking of.
There may be orange blossoms later,
Kind of think that there will,
'Cause she's done something to me
And my heart won't keep still.
Give me one dozen roses,
Put my heart in beside them,
And send them to the one I love.

Refrain

Only You (And You Alone)

Words and Music by Buck Ram and Ande Rand

recorded by The Platters, The Hilltoppers and Franck Pourcel's French Fiddles

Only you
Can make this world seem right,
Only you
Can make the darkness bright.
Only you and you alone
Can thrill me like you do,
And fill my heart with love
For only you.

Only you
Can make this change in me
For it's true,
You are my destiny.
When you hold my hand,
I understand
The magic that you do.
You're my dream come true,
My one and only you.

Our Love

Words and Music by Al Jarreau, Jay Graydon and Tom Canning

recorded by Natalie Cole

There's a land where lovers dream,
Where poets dwell:
We can sail tomorrow.
There is always room for one who wishes well.
There are doubters who
Will be welcome, too.
When you can't afford the fare,
There's a wish to borrow.

Refrain:
Our love,
We must never doubt it.
Our love, when you think about it,
Love like ours will live a thousand years.

Yes, I know you've heard the story without end,
And you're uninspired.
Still, a walk without a wish cannot begin.
If you wish at all, we can conquer all;
Learn to walk and run again
As we chase Goliath.

Refrain

Repeat Verse 1 and Fade

Out of Nowhere

Words by Edward Heyman
Music by Johnny Green

from the Paramount Picture *Dude Ranch*
featured in the film *The Joker Is Wild*
recorded by Guy Lombardo, Frank Sinatra, Lena Horne, Artie Shaw and various other artists

You came to me from out of nowhere,
You took my heart and found it free.
Wonderful dreams, wonderful schemes from nowhere;
Make every hour sweet as a flower for me.

If you should go back to your nowhere,
Leaving me with a memory.
I'll always wait for your return out of nowhere;
Hoping that you'll bring your love to me.

Refrain:
When I least expected
Kindly fate directed
You to make each dream of mine come true.
And if it's clear or raining
There is no explaining
Things just happen and so did you.

Repeat Verses

Penthouse Serenade

Words and Music by Will Jason and Val Burton

a standard recorded by various artists

Picture a penthouse way up in the sky,
With hinges on chimneys for stars to go by;
A sweet slice of heaven for just you and I
When we're alone.

From all of society we'll stay aloof,
And love in propriety there on the roof,
Two heavenly hermits we will be in truth,
When we're alone.

We'll see life's mad pattern,
As we view old Manhattan.
Then we can thank our lucky stars,
That we're living as we are.

In our little penthouse we'll always contrive,
To keep love and romance forever alive,
In view of the Hudson just over the Drive,
When we're alone.

Picnic

Words by Steve Allen
Music by George W. Duning

from the Columbia Technicolor Picture *Picnic*

On a picnic morning,
Without a warning,
I looked at you,
And somehow I knew.

On a day for singing,
My heart went winging,
A picnic grove was our rendezvous.
You and I in the sunshine,
We strolled the fields and farms,
At the last light of evening.
I held you in my arms.

Now when days grow stormy
And lonely for me,
I just recall picnic time with you.

Now when days grow stormy
And lonely for me,
I just recall picnic time with you.

The Power of Love

Words by Mary Susan Applegate and Jennifer Rush
Music by Candy Derouge and Gunther Mende

recorded by Celine Dion

The whispers in the morning,
Of lovers sleeping tight,
Are rolling by like thunder now,
As I look into your eyes.

I hold on to your body,
And feel each move you make.
Your voice is warm and tender,
A love that I could not forsake.

Refrain:
'Cause I'm your lady
And you are my man.
Whenever you reach for me,
I'll do all that I can.

Even though there may be times
It seems I'm far away,
Never wonder where I am
'Cause I am always by your side.

Refrain

We're heading for something,
Somewhere I've never been.
Sometimes I am frightened
But I'm ready to learn
'Bout the power of love.

The sound of your heart beating
Made it clear and suddenly.
The feeling that I can't go on
Is light years away.

Refrain

We're heading for something,
Somewhere I've never been.
Sometimes I'm frightened
But I'm ready to learn
'Bout the power of love.
The power of love.

Precious and Few

Words and Music by Walter D. Nims

recorded by Climax

Precious and few are the moments we two can share;
Quiet and blue like the sky I'm hung over you.
And if I can't find my way back home
It just wouldn't be fair
'Cause precious and few
Are the moments we two can share.

Baby, it's you on my mind, your love is so rare
Being with you is a feeling I just can't compare.
And if I can't hold you in my arms
It just wouldn't be fair,
'Cause precious and few
Are the moments we two can share.

Ribbon in the Sky

Words and Music by Stevie Wonder

recorded by Stevie Wonder

Oh, so long for this night I prayed
That a star would guide you my way
To share with me this special day
Where a ribbon's in the sky for our love.

If allowed, may I touch your hand
And if pleased may I once again,
So that you too will understand
There's a ribbon in the sky for our love.

Doo doo doo...

This is not a coincidence,
And far more than a lucky chance,
But what is that was always meant
Is our ribbon in the sky for our love, love.

We can't lose with God on our side.
We'll find strength in each tear we cry.
From now on it will be you and I
And our ribbon in the sky,
Ribbon in the sky
A ribbon in the sky for our love.

Ooh, ooh...

There's a ribbon in the sky for our love.

Save the Best for Last

Words and Music by Phil Galdston, Jon Lind and Wendy Waldman

recorded by Vanessa Williams

Sometimes the snow comes down in June.
Sometimes the sun goes 'round the moon.
I see the passion in your eyes.
Sometimes it's all a big surprise.

'Cause there was a time when all I did
Was wish you'd tell me this was love.
It's not the way I hoped or how I planned,
But somehow it's enough.

And now we're standing face to face
Isn't this world a crazy place?
Just when I thought our chance had passed,
You go and save the best for last.

All of the nights you came to me
When some silly girl had set you free.
You wondered how you'd make it through.
I wondered what was wrong with you.

'Cause how could you give your love
To someone else and share your dreams
   with me?
Sometimes the very thing you're looking for
Is the one thing you can't see.

But now we're standing face to face,
Isn't this world a crazy place?
Just when I thought our chance had passed
You go and save the best for last.

Sometimes the very thing you're looking for
Is the one thing you can't see.

Sometimes the snow comes down in June.
Sometimes the sun goes 'round the moon.
Just when I thought a chance had passed,
You go and save the best for last.
You went and saved the best for last.

She

Lyric by Herbert Kretzmer
Music by Charles Aznavour

Theme from the BBC/TV Series *Seven Faces of Woman*
featured in the film *Notting Hill*
recorded by Charles Aznavour

She may be the face I can't forget
A trace of pleasure or regret,
May be my treasure or the price I
   have to pay.
She may be the song that summer sings,
May be the chill that autumn brings,
May be a hundred different things
Within the measure of a day.

She may be the beauty or the beast,
May be the famine or the feast,
May turn each day into a heaven or hell.
She may be the mirror of my dream,
A smile reflected in a stream,
She may not be what she may seem
   inside her shell.

She who always seems so happy in a crowd,
Who's eyes can be so private and so proud,
No one's allowed to see them when they cry.
She may be the love that cannot hope to last,
May come to me from shadows of the past
That I'll remember 'til the day I die.

She may be the reason I survive,
The why and wherefore I'm alive,
The one I'll care for through the rough and
   ready years.
Me, I'll take her laughter and her tears
And make them all my souvenirs,
For where she goes I've got to be,
The meaning of my life is she, she, she.

Some Enchanted Evening

Lyrics by Oscar Hammerstein II
Music by Richard Rodgers

from the musical *South Pacific*

Some enchanted evening
You may see a stranger,
You may see a stranger
Across a crowded room.
And somehow you know,
You know even then,
That somewhere you'll see her again and again.

Some enchanted evening
Someone may be laughing,
You may hear her laughing
Across a crowded room—
And night after night,
As strange as it seems,
The sound of her laughter will sing in your dreams.

Who can explain it?
Who can tell you why?
Fools give you reasons—
Wise men never try.

Some enchanted evening
When you find your true love,
When you hear her call you
Across a crowded room,
Then fly to her side
And make her your own,
Or all through your life
You may dream all alone.
Once you have found her,
Never let her go.
Once you have found her,
Never let her go.

Somewhere in the Night

Words and Music by Will Jennings and Richard Kerr

recorded by Barry Manilow

Time, you found time enough to love,
And I found love enough to hold you.
So tonight I'll stir the fire you feel inside
Until the flames of love enfold you.
Layin' beside you, lost in the feeling,
So glad you opened my door.
Come with me, somewhere in the night we will know
Everything lovers can know.
You're my song, music too magic to end,
I'll play you over and over again.
Lovin' so warm, movin' so right,
Closin' our eyes, and feelin' the light,
We'll just go on burnin' bright,
Somewhere in the night.

You'll sleep when the mornin' comes.
And I'll lie and watch you sleepin'.
And you'll smile when you dream about the night,
Like it's a secret you've been keepin'.
Layin' beside you, lost in the feeling,
So glad you opened my door.
You're my song, music too magic to end,
I'll play you over and over again.
Lovin' so warm, movin' so right,
Closin' our eyes and feelin' the light.
We'll just go on burnin' bright,
Somewhere in the night.
We'll just go on burnin' bright,
Somewhere in the night.

Speak Softly, Love (Love Theme)

Words by Larry Kusik
Music by Nino Rota

from the Paramount Picture *The Godfather*
recorded by Andy Williams

Speak softly, love, and hold me warm against your heart.
I feel your words, the tender, trembling moments start.
We're in a world our very own,
Sharing a love that only few have ever known.
Wine colored days warmed by the sun,
Deep velvet nights when we are one.

Speak softly, love, so no one hears us but the sky.
The vows of love we make will live until we die.
My life is yours, and all because
You came into my world with love so softly, love.

Repeat Song

Sweet and Lovely

Words and Music by Gus Arnheim, Charles N. Daniels and Harry Tobias

a standard recorded by various artists

There's sweetness in the call of the woodland dove
As his love song echoes through the trees.
There's sweetness in the rose with its symbol of love,
Floating on a summer breeze.
But nothing can compare to the sweetness
Of the one and only one I love.

Refrain:
Sweet and lovely,
Sweeter than the roses in May.
Sweet and lovely,
Heaven must have sent her my way.
Skies above me
Never were as blue as her eyes,
And she loves me,
Who would want a sweeter surprise.
When she nestles in my arms so tenderly,
There's a thrill that words cannot express.
In my heart a song of love is taunting me,
Melody haunting me.
Sweet and lovely,
Sweeter than the roses in May,
And she loves me,
There is nothing more I can say.

Repeat Refrain

The Sweetest Days

Words and Music by Jon Lind, Wendy Waldman and Phil Galdston

recorded by Vanessa Williams

You and I in this moment,
Holding the night so close,
Hanging on, still unbroken
While outside the thunder rolls.
Listen now, you can hear my heart beat
Warm against life's bitter cold.
These are the days,
The sweetest days we'll know.

There are times that scare me.
We'll rattle the house like the wind,
Both of us so unbending.
We battle the fear within.
All the while life is rushing by us.
Hold it now and don't let go.
These are the days,
The sweetest days we'll know.

So, we'll whisper a dream here in the darkness,
Watching the stars till their gone.
And when even the memories have all faded away,
These days gone on and on.
Listen, you can hear my heart beat.
Hold me now and don't let go.
(These are the days)
Every day is the sweetest day we'll know.
(These are the days)
The sweetest days we'll ever know.

Tenderly

Lyric by Jack Lawrence
Music by Walter Gross

from the film *Torch Song*
a standard recorded by various artists

The evening breeze caressed the trees tenderly.
The trembling trees embraced the breeze tenderly.
Then you and I came wandering by,
And lost in a sigh were we.

The shore was kissed by sea and mist tenderly.
I can't forget how two hearts met breathlessly.
Your arms opened wide and closed me inside;
You took my lips, you took my love so tenderly.

Thank God I Found You

Words and Music by Mariah Carey, James Harris III and Terry Lewis

recorded by Mariah Carey featuring Joe & 98 Degrees

Female:
I would give up ev'rything
Before I'd separate myself from you.
After so much suffering,
I fin'lly found unvarnished truth.
I was all by myself for the longest time,
So cold inside,
And the hurt from the heartache
   would not subside;
I felt like dying, until you saved my life.

Refrain:
Thank God I found you.
I was lost without you.
My ev'ry wish and ev'ry dream
Somehow became reality
When you brought the sunlight,
Completed my whole life.
I'm overwhelmed with gratitude,
'Cause baby, I'm so thankful I found you.

Male:
And I would give you ev'rything;
There's nothing in this world I wouldn't do
To ensure your happiness.
I'll cherish ev'ry part of you
'Cause without you beside me I can't survive;
Don't want to try.
If you're keeping me warm each and
   ev'ry night,
I'll be all right,
'Cause I need you in my life.

Refrain

Female:
See, I was so desolate
Before you came to me.
Looking back,

Male:
I guess

Both:
It shows that we were destined to shine
After the rain to appreciate
The gift of what we have.

Male:
And I'd go through it all over again
To be able to feel this way.

Thank God I found you.
I was lost without you.
My ev'ry wish and ev'ry dream
Somehow became reality
When you brought the sunlight,
Completed my whole life.
I'm overwhelmed with gratitude;
Sweet baby, I'm so thankful I found you.
Thank God I found you.
I was lost without you.
I'm overwhelmed with gratitude;
My baby, I'm so thankful I found you.

Female:
I'm overwhelmed with gratitude;
My baby, I'm so thankful I found you.

That Old Black Magic

Words by Johnny Mercer
Music by Harold Arlen

from the Paramount Picture *Star Spangled Rhythm*
a standard recorded by Glenn Miller, Frank Sinatra, Louis Prima and other artists
featured in the films *Here Come the Waves*, *When You're Smiling*,
Meet Danny Wilson, *Senior Prom*, *Bustop*

That old black magic has me in its spell.
That old black magic that you weave so well.
Those icy fingers up and down my spine.
The same old witchcraft when your eyes meet mine.
The same old tingle that I feel inside
And then that elevator starts its ride
And down and down I go,
'Round and 'round I go
Like a leaf that's caught in the tide.

I should stay away but what can I do
I hear your name and I'm aflame,
Aflame with such a burning desire
That only your kiss can put out the fire.
For you're the lover I have waited for.
The mate that fate had me created for
And every time your lips meet mine
Darling down and down I go,
'Round and 'round I go in a spin,
Loving the spin I'm in
Under that old black magic called love!

That's What Love Is All About

Words and Music by Michael Bolton and Eric Kaz

recorded by Michael Bolton

There was a time,
We thought our dream was over,
When you and I had surely reached the end.
Still, here we are.
The flame is strong as ever.
All because we both kept holding on.
We know we can weather any storm.

Refrain:
Baby that's what love is all about,
Two hearts that found a way somehow
To keep the fire burning.
It's something we could never live without.
If it takes forever, we can work it out
Beyond a shadow of a doubt.
Baby, that's what love is all about.

As the time goes by,
We learned to rediscover
The reason why this dream of ours survives.
Through thick and thin,
We're destined for each other,
Knowing we can reach the other side,
Far beyond the mountains of our pride.

Refrain

Oh, ridin' the good times is easy.
The hard times can tear you apart.
There'll be times in your heart
When the feelin' is gone,
But ya keep on believing
And ya' keep holdin' on.

Refrain

There Is No Greater Love

Words by Marty Symes
Music by Isham Jones

a standard recorded by various artists

The sunshine loves the flowers,
The flowers love the dew;
There are many diff'rent kinds of love, it's true.
The stars all love the moonbeams
Away up in the blue,
But there never was a love like mine for you.

Refrain:
There is no greater love than what I feel for you,
No greater love, no heart so true.
There is no greater thrill than what you bring to me,
No sweeter song than what you sing to me.
You're the sweetest thing I have ever known,
And to think that you are mine alone!
There is no greater love in all the world, it's true,
No greater love than what I feel for you.

Repeat Refrain

Three Little Words

Lyric by Bert Kalmar
Music by Harry Ruby

from the Motion Picture *Check and Double Check*

Three words in my dictionary I could never see,
But to my vocabulary I've added those three.
I'm waiting for someone to say them to me.

Refrain:
Three little words,
Oh, what I'd give for that wonderful phrase.
To hear those three little words,
That's all I'd live for the rest of my days.
And what I feel in my heart, they tell sincerely,
No other words can tell it half so clearly.
Three little words, eight little letters,
Which simply mean, "I love you"!

I used to pay no attention whenever I'd hear
Some lonesome Romeo mention, "I love you, my dear."
Now I want to hear it each time you draw near.

Refrain

Through the Years

Words and Music by Steve Dorff and Marty Panzer

recorded by Kenny Rogers

I can't remember when you weren't there,
When I didn't care for anyone but you,
I swear we've been through everything there is,
Can't imagine anything we've missed.
Can't imagine anything the two of us can't do.

Through the years
You've never let me down,
You've turned my life around.
The sweetest days I've found
I've found with you.

Through the years,
I've never been afraid,
I've loved the life we've made,
And I'm so glad I've stayed
Right here with you
Through the years.

I can't remember what I used to do,
Who I trusted
Who I listened to before.
I swear you've taught me everything I know,
Can't imagine needing someone so.

Through the years,
I've never been afraid,
I've loved the life we've made,
And I'm so glad I've stayed
Right here with you
Through the years.

Till

Words by Carl Sigman
Music by Charles Danvers

recorded by various artists

Till the moon deserts the sky,
Till all the seas run dry;
Till then I'll worship you.
Till the tropic sun grows cold,
Till this young world grows old,
My darling, I'll adore you.
You are my reason to live;
All that I own I would give
Just to have you adore me.
Till the rivers flow upstream,
Till lovers cease to dream,
Till then, I'm yours, be mine.

Till the End of Time

(Based on Chopin's Polonaise)
Words and Music by Buddy Kaye and Ted Mossman

from *Till the End of Time*

Till the end of time,
Long as stars are in the blue,
Long as there's a spring, a bird to sing,
I'll go on loving you.
Till the end of time,
Long as roses bloom in May,
My love for you will grow deeper
With ev'ry passing day.
Till the wells run dry
And each mountain disappears,
I'll be there for you, to care for you
Through laughter and through tears.
So take my heart in sweet surrender
And tenderly say that I'm
The one you'll love and live for
Till the end of time.

Till We Two Are One

Words by Tom Glazer
Music by Larry and Billy Martin

Take my lips and give me yours,
Take my arms and give me yours,
Take my heart and give me yours,
Till we two are one.
Just one kiss, if we should dare,
Just one love for us to share,
Just one ecstasy is there
Till we two are one.
There could be heavenly dreams we take and give for
Thrillingly, willingly, moments we live for.
Take my love and give me yours,
Take my life and give me yours,
Take my soul and give me yours,
Till we two are one.

A Time for Us (Love Theme)

Words by Larry Kusik and Eddie Snyder
Music by Nino Rota

from the Paramount Picture *Romeo and Juliet*
recorded by Andy Williams

A time for us, someday there'll be,
When chains are torn by courage born
Of a love that's free.
A time when dreams, so long denied
Can flourish, as we unveil the love we now must hide.

A time for us at last to see,
A life worthwhile for you and me.
And with our love through tears and thorns,
We will endure as we pass surely through every storm.
A time for us someday there'll be,
A new world, a world of shining hope for you and me.

To Each His Own

Words and Music by Jay Livingston and Ray Evans

from the Paramount Picture *To Each His Own*
from the Paramount Picture *The Conversation*
recorded by Monty Alexander

Wise men have shown
Life is no good alone.
Day needs night, flowers need light,
I need you, I need you.

A rose must remain with the sun and the rain
Or its lovely promise won't come true.
To each his own, to each his own,
And my own is you.

What good is a song if the words just don't belong,
And a dream must be a dream for two.
No good alone, to each his own,
For me there's you.

If a flame is to grow there must be a glow,
To open the door there's a key.
I need you, I know, I can't let you go.
Your touch means too much to me.

Two lips must insist on two more to be kissed
Or they'll never know what love can do.
To each his own, I've found my own
One and only you.

To Love Again

(Based on Chopin's E-flat Nocturne)
Words by Ned Washington
Music by Morris Stoloff and George Sidney

Theme from the film *The Eddy Duchin Story*
recorded by The Four Aces

No heart should refuse love.
How lucky are the ones who choose love.
And if we should lose love,
We have the right to love again.
In the world full of faces
So few ever find their places.
In many cases, hearts have lost their way.
Don't live in the past, dear.
For you and me the die is cast, dear.
But if love won't last, dear,
We have the right to love again.

To Love You More

Words and Music by David Foster and Junior Miles

recorded by Celine Dion

Take me back into the arms I love.
Need me like you did before.
Touch me once again
And remember when
There was no one that you wanted more.

Don't go, you know you'll break my heart.
She won't love you like I will.
I'm just the one who'll stay,
When she walks away,
And you know I'll be standing here still.

Refrain:
I'll be waiting for you,
Here inside my heart.
I'm the one who wants to love you more.
You will see I can give you
Everything you need.
Let me be the one to love you more.

See me as if you never know.
Hold me so you can't let go.
Just believe in me.
I will make you see
All the things that your heart needs to know.

Refrain

And some way, all the love that we had can
    be saved.
Whatever it takes, we'll find a way.
I will make you see
All the things that your heart needs to know.

I'll be waiting for you,
Here inside my heart.
I'm the one who wants to love you more.
Can't you see I can give you
Everything you need.
Let me be the one to love you more.

Tonight, I Celebrate My Love

Music by Michael Masser
Lyric by Gerry Goffin

recorded by Peabo Bryson & Roberta Flack

Tonight, I celebrate my love for you;
It seems that natural thing to do.
Tonight, no one's gonna find us,
We'll have the world behind us,
When I make love to you.

Tonight, I celebrate my love for you;
And hope that deep inside you feel it too.
Tonight, our spirits will be climbing
To a sky lit up with diamonds
When I make love to you
Tonight.

Refrain:
Tonight, I celebrate my love for you
And the midnight sun
Is gonna come shining through.
Tonight, there'll be no distance between us.
What I want most to do
Is to get close to you tonight.

Tonight, I celebrate my love for you.
And soon this old world will seem brand new.
Tonight, we will both discover
How friends turn into lovers,
When I make love to you.

Refrain

Top of the World

Words and Music by John Bettis and Richard Carpenter

recorded by The Carpenters

Such a feelin's comin' over me,
There is wonder in most everything I see,
Not a cloud in the sky got the sun in my eyes,
And I won't be surprised if it's a dream.
Everything I want the world to be,
Is now coming true especially for me,
And the reason is clear,
It's because you are here,
You're the nearest thing to heaven that I've seen.

Refrain:
I'm on the top of the world
Lookin' down on creation
And the only explanation I can find,
Is the love that I've found,
Ever since you've been around,
Your love's put me at the top of the world.

Something in the wind has learned my name,
And it's tellin' me that things are not the same,
In the leaves on the trees and touch of the breeze,
There's a pleasin' sense of happiness for me.
There is only one wish on my mind,
When this day is through I hope that I will find,
That tomorrow will be just the same for you and me,
All I need will be mine if you are here.

Refrain

The Touch of Your Lips

Words and Music by Ray Noble

a standard recorded by various artists

When troubles get me, cares beset me
And won't let me go,
I turn to you for consolation.
There I find new peace of mind;
To leave behind my woe,
I turn to you as I shall always do.

Refrain:
The touch of your lips upon my brow;
Your lips that are cool and sweet;
Such tenderness lies in their soft caress,
My heart forgets to beat.
The touch of your hands upon my head,
The love in your eyes a-shine;
And now at last the moment divine,
The touch of your lips on mine.

True Love

Words and Music by Cole Porter

from the film *High Society*
recorded by Bing Crosby & Grace Kelly, and various other artists

Sun-tanned, wind-blown
Honeymooners at last alone,
Feeling far above par,
Oh, how lucky we are
While

I give to you and you give to me
True love, true love.
So, on and on it will always be
True love, true love.
For you and I
Have a guardian angel on high
With nothing to do
But to give to you and to give to me
Love, forever true.

Truly, Madly, Deeply

Words and Music by Daniel Jones and Darren Hayes

recorded by Savage Garden

I'll be your dream, I'll be your wish,
I'll be your fantasy.
I'll be your hope,
I'll be your love
Be everything that you need.
I'll love you more with every breath,
Truly, madly, deeply do.
I will be strong, I will be faithful,
'Cause I'm counting on a new beginning.
A reason for living,
A deeper meaning, yeah.

Refrain:
I want to stand with you on a mountain,
I want to bathe with you in the sea.
I want to lay like this forever,
Until the sky falls down on me.

And then the stars are shining brightly
In the velvet sky,
I'll make a wish and send it to heaven,
Then make you want to cry
The tears of joy
For all the pleasure in the certainty,
That we're surrounded by the comfort
And protection of the highest powers,
In lonely hours,
The tears devour you.

Refrain

Oh, can you see it baby?
You don't have to close your eyes
'Cause it's standing right beside you, ooh.
All that you need will surely come.

Repeat Verse 1

Refrain

Twilight Time

Lyric by Buck Ram
Music by Morty Nevins and Al Nevins

recorded by The Platters

Heavenly shades of night are falling,
It's twilight time.
Out of the mist your voice is calling,
It's twilight time.
When purple colored curtains mark the end of day,
I hear you, my dear, at twilight time.

Deepening shadows gather splendor,
As day is done.
Fingers of night will soon surrender
The setting sun.
I count the moments, darling till you're here with me.
Together, at last at twilight time.

Here in the afterglow of day
We keep our rendezvous beneath the blue.
Here in the sweet and same old way
I fall in love again as I did then.

Deep in the dark your kiss will thrill me
Like days of old.
Lighting the spark of love that fills me
With dreams untold.
Each day I pray for evening just to be with you,
Together at last at twilight time.

Two Sleepy People

Words by Frank Loesser
Music by Hoagy Carmichael

from the Paramount Motion Picture *Thanks for the Memory*

Here we are, out of cigarettes,
Holding hands and yawning, look how late it gets.
Two sleepy people, by dawn's early light,
And too much in love to say "Good night."

Here we are in the cozy chair,
Picking on a wishbone from the Frigidaire,
Two sleepy people with nothing to say
And too much in love to break away.

Do you remember the nights
We used to linger in the hall?
Father didn't like you at all.
Do you remember the reason
Why we married in the fall?
To rent this little nest and get a bit of rest.

Well, here we are just about the same,
Foggy little fella, drowsy little dame,
Two sleepy people, by dawn's early light,
And too much in love to say "Good night."

Unchained Melody

Lyric by Hy Zaret
Music by Alex North

from the film *Unchained*
recorded by Les Baxter, Al Hibbler, Roy Hamilton, The Righteous Brothers
featured in the film *Ghost*

Oh, my love, my darling,
I've hungered for your touch,
A long, lonely time.
Time goes by so slowly
And time can do so much,
Are you still mine?
I need your love, I need your love,
God speed your love to me!

Lonely rivers flow to the sea,
To the sea,
To the open arms
Of the sea.

Lonely rivers sigh,
"Wait for me,
Wait for me!"
I'll be coming home,
Wait for me.

Repeat Verse 1

Up Where We Belong

Words by Will Jennings
Music by Buffy Sainte-Marie and Jack Nitzsche

from the film *Up Where We Belong*
from the Paramount Picture *An Officer and a Gentleman*
recorded by Joe Cocker & Jennifer Warnes

Who knows what tomorrow brings;
In a world, few hearts survive.
All I know is the way I feel.
When it's real,
I keep it alive.
The road is long.
There are mountains in our way,
But we climb a step every day.

Refrain:
Love lift us up where we belong,
Where the eagle cry
On a mountain high.
Love lift us up where we belong,
Far from the world we know;
Up where the clear winds blow.

Some hang on to "used to be,"
Live their lives looking behind.
All we have is here and now;
All our life, out there to find.
The road is long.
There are mountains in our way,
But we climb them a step every day.

Refrain

Time goes by, no time to cry,
Life's you and I,
Alive,
Today.

Refrain

Valentine

Words and Music by Jack Kugell and Jim Brickman

recorded by Jim Brickman with Martina McBride

If there were no words,
No way to speak,
I would still hear you.
If there were no tears,
No way to feel inside,
I'd still feel for you.

Refrain:
And even if the sun refused to shine,
Even if romance ran out of rhyme,
You would sill have my heart
Until the end of time.
You're all I need my love,
My valentine.

All of my life,
I have been waiting for all you give to me.
You've opened my eyes and shown me
How to love unselfishly.
I've dreamed of this a thousand times before,
But in my dreams I couldn't love you more.
I will give you my heart until the end of time.
'Cause all I need is you,
My valentine.

Refrain

My valentine.

The Very Thought of You

Words and Music by Ray Noble

a standard recorded by Ray Noble, Benny Carter, Billie Holiday and various other artists

The very thought of you,
And I forget to do
The little ordinary things
That everyone ought to do.

I'm living in a kind of daydream,
I'm happy as a king,
And foolish though it may seem,
To me that's everything.

The mere idea of you,
The longing here for you,
You'll never know how slow
The moments go
'Til I'm near to you.

I see your face in every flower;
Your eyes in stars above.
It's just the thought of you,
The very thought of you, my love.

We're in This Love Together

Words and Music by Keith Stegall and Roger Murrah

recorded by Al Jarreau

It's a diamond ring, it's a precious thing,
And we never want to lose it.
It's like a favorite song that we love to sing,
Every time we hear the music.

Refrain:
And we're in this love together;
We got the kind that'll last forever.
We're in this love together;
And like berries on the vine
It gets sweeter all the time.

It's like a rainy night and candle light,
And ooh, it's so romantic.
We got the whole thing working out so right,
And it's just the way we planned it.

Refrain

We're in this love together:
We got the kind that'll last forever.
We're in this love together;
We got the kind that'll last forever and evermore.

We've Only Just Begun

Words and Music by Roger Nichols and Paul Williams

recorded by The Carpenters

We've only just begun to live,
White lace and promises,
A kiss for luck and we're on our way.

Before the rising sun we fly,
So many roads to choose,
We start out walking and learn to run.

Refrain:
And yes, we've just begun.
Sharing horizons that are new to us,
Watching the signs along the way.
Talking it over just the two of us,
Working together day to day, together.

And when the evening comes we smile,
So much of life ahead,
We'll find a place where there's room to grow.

Refrain

And when the evening comes we smile,
So much of life ahead,
We'll find a place where there's room to grow.

And yes, we've just begun.

What the World Needs Now Is Love

Lyric by Hal David
Music by Burt Bacharach

recorded by Jackie DeShannon

Refrain:
What the world needs now is love, sweet love,
It's the only thing that there's just too little of.
What the world needs now is love, sweet love,
No, not just for some, but for everyone.

Lord, we don't need another mountain,
There are mountains and hillsides enough to climb;
There are oceans and rivers enough to cross,
Enough to last, till the end of time.

Refrain

Lord, we don't need another meadow,
There are cornfields and wheat fields enough to grow;
There are sunbeams and moonbeams enough to shine,
Oh, listen, Lord, if you want to know.

Refrain

No not just for some,
Oh, but just for everyone.

When I Fall in Love

Words by Edward Heyman
Music by Victor Young

from the film *One Minute to Zero*
recorded by Nat "King" Cole, Doris Day, The Lettermen, Celine Dion & Clive Griffin
featured in the TriStar Motion Picture *Sleepless in Seattle*

When I fall in love
It will be forever,
Or I'll never fall in love.

In a restless world like this is,
Love is ended before it's begun,
And too many moonlight kisses
Seem to cool in the warmth of the sun.

When I give my heart
It will be completely,
Or I'll never give my heart.

And the moment I can feel
That you feel that way too
Is when I fall in love with you.

When Love Is All There Is (Wedding Story)

Music and Lyrics by Chris Curtis

Theme from TLC's *A Wedding Story*

When love is all there is, you don't remember
The moments when you haven't seen her face,
And something in your heart makes you surrender
To a feeling that your dreams could not replace.
When love is all you know, you never listen
To all the cautious words that people say;
The only thing you have is your ambition
To find a way to love her ev'ry day.

When all the thoughts you have all lead up to her,
Then moments could last for a year or two.
And when the spark of youth someday surrenders,
I will have your hand to see me through.
The years may come and go, but there's one thing I know:
Love is all there is when I'm with you.
The years may come and go, but one thing that I know:
Love is all there is when I'm with you.

When You Say Nothing at All

Words and Music by Paul Overstreet and Don Schlitz

featured in the film *Notting Hill*
recorded by Keith Whitley, Alison Krauss & Union Station

It's amazing how you can speak right to my heart.
Without saying a word you can light up the dark.
Try as I may I could never explain
What I hear when you don't say a thing.

Refrain:
The smile on your face lets me know that you need me.
There's truth in your eyes saying you'll never leave me.
A touch of your hand says you'll catch me if ever I fall.
Now you say it's best when you say nothing at all.

All day long I can hear people talking out loud,
But when you hold me near you drown out the crowd.
Old Mister Webster could never define
What's being said between your heart and mine.

Refrain

Where Do I Begin (Love Theme)

Words by Carl Sigman
Music by Francis Lai

from the Paramount Picture *Love Story*
recorded by Andy Williams, Henry Mancini, Francis Lai

Where do I begin,
To tell the story of how great a love can be,
The sweet love story that is older than the sea,
The simple truth about the love she brings to me?
Where do I start?

With her first hello,
She gave a meaning to this empty world of mine;
There'll never be another love, another time;
She came into my life and made the living fine.
She fills my heart.

She fills my heart
With very special things,
With angel songs,
With wild imaginings,
She fills my soul
With so much love
That anywhere I go
I'm never lonely.
With her along,
Who could be lonely?
I reach for her hand,
It's always there.

How long does it last?
Can love be measured by the hours in a day?
I have no answers now, but this much I can say:
I know I'll need her 'til the stars all burn away
And she'll be there.

Wish Me a Rainbow

Words and Music by Jay Livingston and Ray Evans

Theme from the Paramount Picture *This Property Is Condemned*

Wish me a rainbow and wish me a star.
All this you can give me, wherever you are,
And dreams for my pillow and stars for my eyes,
And a masquerade ball where our love wins first prize.
Wish me red roses and yellow balloons,
And black sequins whirling to gay dancing tunes.
I want all those treasures, the most you can give.
So wish me a rainbow as long as I live!
All my tomorrows depend on your love.
So wish me a rainbow from above!

Wish me a rainbow and wish me a star.
All this you can give me, wherever you are,
And dreams for my pillow and stars for my eyes,
And a masquerade ball where our love wins first prize.
Wish me red roses and yellow balloons,
And carousels whirling to gay dancing tunes.
I want all those treasures, the most you can give.
So wish me a rainbow as long as I live!
All my tomorrows depend on your love.
So wish me a rainbow from above!

Witchcraft

Lyric by Carolyn Leigh
Music by Cy Coleman

recorded by Frank Sinatra

Shades of old Lucretia Borgia!
There's a devil in you tonight
'N' although my heart adores ya
My head says it ain't right,
Right to let you make advances, oh no!
Under normal circumstances, I'd go but oh!

Those fingers in my hair,
That sly, come hither stare
That strips my conscience bare,
It's witchcraft.

And I've got no defense for it,
The heat is too intense for it,
What good would common sense for it do?
'Cause it's witchcraft!
Wicked witchcraft.
And although I know it's strictly taboo.
When you arouse the need in me,
My heart says, "Yes, indeed" in me.
"Proceed with what you're leadin' me to!"
It's such an ancient pitch
But one I wouldn't switch
'Cause there's no nicer witch than you!

With These Hands

Lyric by Benny Davis
Music by Abner Silver

With these hands I will cling to you,
I'm yours forever and a day.
With these hands I will bring to you
A tender love as warm as May.
With this heart I will sing to you,
Long after stars have lost their glow,
And with these hands I'll provide for you;
Should there be a stormy sea,
I'll turn the tide for you,
And I'll never, no, I'll never let you go.

Wonderful Tonight

Words and Music by Eric Clapton

recorded by Eric Clapton

It's late in the evening; she's wondering what clothes to wear.
She puts on her makeup and brushes her long blonde hair.
And then she asks me, "Do I look all right?"
And I say, "Yes, you look wonderful tonight."

We go to a party, and everyone turns to see
This beautiful lady is walking around with me.
And then she asks me, "Do you feel all right?"
And I say, "Yes, I feel wonderful tonight."

I feel wonderful because I see the love light in your eyes.
Then the wonder of it all is that you just don't realize
How much I love you.

It's time to go home now, and I've got an aching head.
So I give her the car keys, and she helps me to bed.
And then I tell her, as I turn out the light, I say,
"My darling, you are wonderful tonight.
Oh, my darling, you are wonderful tonight."

You and I

Words and Music by Stevie Wonder

recorded by Stevie Wonder

Here we are,
On earth together, you and I.
God has made us fall in love, it's true.
I've really found someone like you.
Will it stay,
The love you feel for me?
Will it say,
That you will be by my side to see me through,
Until my life is through?
Well, in my mind,
We can conquer the world.
In love, you and I.
You and I.
You and I.

I am glad,
At least in my life I found someone,
That may not be here forever to see me through.
But I found strength in you.
I only pray,
That I have shown you a brighter day,
Because that's all that I am living for, you see.
Don't worry what happens to me,
'Cause in my mind
You will stay here always.
In love, you and I.
You and I.
You and I.

You Are So Beautiful

Words and Music by Billy Preston and Bruce Fisher

recorded by Joe Cocker

You are so beautiful to me.
You are so beautiful to me.
Can't you see you're everything that I hope for
And what's more, you're everything I need.
You are so beautiful, baby, to me.

You're everything that I hope for
And what's more, you're everything I need.
You are so beautiful, baby, to me.

Such joy and happiness you bring.
(I wanna thank you babe.)
Such joy and happiness you bring,
Just like a dream.
You're the guiding light shinin' in the night,
You're heaven still to me.
(Hey baby,)

You are so beautiful.
You are so beautiful.

You Are the Sunshine of My Life

Words and Music by Stevie Wonder

recorded by Stevie Wonder

You are the sunshine of my life,
That's why I'll always be around.
You are the apple of my eye.
Forever you'll stay in my heart.

I feel like this is the beginning,
'Though I've loved you for a million years.
And if I thought our love was ending,
I'd find myself, drowning in my own tears.

You are the sunshine of my life,
That's why I'll always stay around.
You are the apple of my eye.
Forever you'll stay in my heart.

You must have known that I was lonely,
Because you came to my rescue.
And I know that this must be heaven;
How could so much love, be inside of you?

Repeat Verse 1 and Fade

You Better Go Now

Words by Bickley Reichner
Music by Robert Graham

from the musical *New Faces of 1936*
a standard recorded by various artists

You better go now
Because I like you much too much,
You have a way with you.
You ought to know now
Just why I like you very much.
The night was gay with you.

There's the moon above,
And it gives my heart a lot of swing.
In your eyes there's love,
And the way I feel it must be spring.
I want you so now,
You have the lips I love to touch;
You better go now,
You better go because I like you much too much.

You Brought a New Kind of Love to Me

Words and Music by Sammy Fain, Irving Kahal and Pierre Norman

from the Paramount Picture *The Big Pond*
a standard recorded by Maurice Chevalier and various other artists
from the film *New York, New York*

If the nightingales could sing like you,
They'd sing sweeter than they do,
For you've brought a new kind of love to me.
If the sandman brought me dreams of you,
I'd want to sleep my whole life through;
For you've brought a new kind of love to me.

I know that I'm the slave,
You're the queen, but still you can understand,
That underneath it all,
You're a maid and I am only a man.

I would work and slave the whole day through,
If I could hurry home to you,
For you've brought a new kind of love to me.

You Needed Me

Words and Music by Randy Goodrum

recorded by Anne Murray

I cried a tear, you wiped it dry.
I was confused, you cleared my mind.
I sold my soul, you bought it back for me
And held me up and gave me dignity.
Somehow you needed me.

Refrain:
You gave me strength to stand alone again
To face the world out on my own again
You put me high upon a pedestal
So high that I can almost see eternity.
You needed me. You needed me;

And I can't believe it's you, I can't believe it's true.
I needed you and you were there
And I'll never leave. Why should I leave?
I'd be a fool
'Cause I've finally found someone
Who really cares.

You held my hand when it was cold.
When I was lost, you took me home.
You gave me hope, when I was at the end,
And turned my lies back into truth again.
You even called me friend.

Refrain

You'd Be So Nice to Come Home To

Words and Music by Cole Porter

from the musical *Something to Shout About*
a standard recorded by various artists

It's not that you're fairer
Than a lot of girls just as pleasin',
That I doff my hat as a worshipper at your shrine,
It's not that you're rarer
Than asparagus out of season,
No, my darling, this is reason
Why you've got to be mine:

Refrain:
You'd be so nice to come home to,
You'd be so nice by the fire,
While the breeze, on high, sang a lullaby,
You'd be all that I could desire,
Under stars, chilled by the winter,
Under an August moon,
Burning above,
You'd be so nice,
You'd be paradise to come home to and love.

Refrain

You'll Be in My Heart (Pop Version)

Words and Music by Phil Collins

from Walt Disney Pictures' *Tarzan*™
recorded by Phil Collins

Come stop your crying; it will be all right.
Just take my hand, hold it tight.
I will protect you from all around you.
I will be here; don't you cry.

For one so small you seem so strong.
My arms will hold you, keep you
   safe and warm.
This bond between us can't be broken.
I will be here; don't you cry.

Refrain:
'Cause you'll be in my heart,
Yes, you'll be in my heart,
From this day on now and forever more.

You'll be in my heart,
No matter what they say.
You'll be here in my heart always.

Why can't they understand the way we feel?
They just don't trust what they can't explain.
I know we're different, but deep inside us,
We're not that different at all.
And...

Refrain

Don't listen to them,
'Cause what do they know?
We need each other to have, to hold.
They'll see in time,
I know.

When destiny calls you
You must be strong.
It may not be with you,
But you've got to hold on.
They'll see in time, I know.
We'll show them together,
'Cause you'll be in my heart.
Believe me, you'll be in my heart.

I'll be there from this day on,
Now and forevermore.
You'll be in my heart,
(You'll be here in my heart.)
No matter what they say.
(I'll be with you.)
You'll be here in my heart,
(I'll be there.)
Always.

I'll be with you.
I'll be there for you always,
Always and always.
Just look over your shoulder.
Just look over your shoulder.
Just look over you shoulder;
I'll be there always.

You're the Inspiration

Words and Music by Peter Cetera and David Foster

recorded by Chicago

You know our love was meant to be
The kind of love that lasts forever.
And I want you here with me
From tonight until the end of time.
You should know everywhere I go;
Always on my mind, in my heart,
In my soul, baby.

Refrain:
You're the meaning of my life,
You're the inspiration.
You bring feeling to my life,
You're the inspiration.

Wanna have you near me,
I wanna have you hear me saying
No one needs you more than I need you.
(No one needs you more than I.)

And I know (yes, I know)
That it's plain to see;
We're so in love when we're together.
Now I know (now I know)
That I need you here with me
From tonight to the end of time.
You should know everywhere I go;
Always on my mind, you're in my heart,
In my soul.

Refrain

Wanna have you near me,
I wanna have you hear me say yeah,
No one needs you more than I need you.
You're the meaning of my life,
You're the inspiration.
You bring feeling to my life,
You're the inspiration.

When you love somebody:
(Till the end of time;)
When you love somebody
(Always on my mind.)
No one needs you more than I.

You've Made Me So Very Happy

Words and Music by Berry Gordy, Frank E. Wilson, Brenda Holloway and Patrice Holloway

recorded by Brenda Holloway; Blood, Sweat & Tears

I lost at love before,
Got mad and closed the door.
But you said try just once more.
I chose you for the one,
Now I'm having so much fun.
You treated me so kind,
I'm about to lose my mind.
You made me so very happy,
I'm so glad you came into my life.

The others were untrue,
But when it came to lovin' you,
I'd spend my whole life with you.
'Cause you came and you took control,
You touched my very soul.
You always showed me that
Loving you was where it's at.
You made me so very happy,
I'm so glad you came into my life.

I love you so much, it seems
That you're even in my dreams.
I hear you calling me.
I'm so in love with you,
All I ever want to do is
Thank you, baby.

You made me so very happy,
I'm so glad you came into my life.
You made me so very happy,
I'm so glad you came into my life.

Yours (Cuando se quiere de veras)

Words by Albert Gamse and Jack Sherr
Music by Gonzalo Roig

Yours till the stars lose their glory!
Yours till the birds fail to sing!
Yours to the end of life's story,
This pledge to you, dear, I bring!
Yours in the gray of December
Here or on far distant shores!
I've never loved anyone the way I love you!
How could I?
When I was born to be just yours.

Artist Index

Songwriter Index

More Collections from The Lyric Library

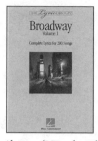

BROADWAY VOLUME I

An invaluable collection of lyrics to 200 top Broadway tunes, including: All at Once You Love Her • All I Ask of You • And All That Jazz • Any Dream Will Do • As Long As He Needs Me • At the End of the Day • Autumn in New York • Bali Ha'i • Bewitched • Cabaret • Castle on a Cloud • Climb Ev'ry Mountain • Comedy Tonight • Don't Rain on My Parade • Everything's Coming up Roses • Hello, Dolly! • I Could Have Danced All Night • I Dreamed a Dream • I Remember It Well • If I Were a Bell • It's the Hard-Knock Life • Let Me Entertain You • Mame • My Funny Valentine • Oklahoma • Seasons of Love • September Song • Seventy Six Trombones • Shall We Dance? • Springtime for Hitler • Summer Nights • Tomorrow • Try to Remember • Unexpected Song • What I Did for Love • With One Look • You'll Never Walk Alone • (I Wonder Why?) You're Just in Love • and more.

_____00240201 ....$14.95

BROADWAY VOLUME II

200 more favorite Broadway lyrics (with no duplication from Volume I): Ain't Misbehavin' • All of You • Another Op'nin', Another Show • As If We Never Said Goodbye • Beauty School Dropout • The Best of Times • Bring Him Home • Brotherhood of Man • Camelot • Close Every Door • Consider Yourself • Do-Re-Mi • Edelweiss • Getting to Know You • Have You Met Miss Jones? • I Loved You Once in Silence • I'm Flying • If Ever I Would Leave You • The Impossible Dream (The Quest) • It Only Takes a Moment • The Lady Is a Tramp • The Last Night of the World • A Little More Mascara • Lost in the Stars • Love Changes Everything • Me and My Girl • Memory • My Heart Belongs to Daddy • On a Clear Day (You Can See Forever) • On My Own • People • Satin Doll • The Sound of Music • Sun and Moon • The Surrey with the Fringe on Top • Unusual Way (In a Very Unusual Way) • We Kiss in a Shadow • We Need a Little Christmas • Who Will Buy? • Wishing You Were Somehow Here Again • Younger Than Springtime • and more.

_____00240205 ....$14.95

CHRISTMAS

200 lyrics to the most loved Christmas songs of all time, including: Angels We Have Heard on High • Auld Lang Syne • Away in a Manger • Baby, It's Cold Outside • The Chipmunk Song • The Christmas Shoes • The Christmas Song (Chestnuts Roasting on an Open Fire) • Christmas Time Is Here • Do They Know It's Christmas? • Do You Hear What I Hear • Feliz Navidad • The First Noel • Frosty the Snow Man • The Gift • God Rest Ye Merry, Gentlemen • Goin' on a Sleighride • Grandma Got Run over by a Reindeer • Happy Xmas (War Is Over) • He Is Born, the Holy Child (Il Est Ne, Le Divin Enfant) • The Holly and the Ivy • A Holly Jolly Christmas • (There's No Place Like) Home for the Holidays • I Heard the Bells on Christmas Day • I Wonder As I Wander • I'll Be Home for Christmas • I've Got My Love to Keep Me Warm • In the Bleak Midwinter • It Came upon the Midnight Clear • It's Beginning to Look like Christmas • It's Just Another New Year's Eve • Jingle Bells • Joy to the World • Mary, Did You Know? • Merry Christmas, Darling • The Most Wonderful Time of the Year • My Favorite Things • Rudolph the Red-Nosed Reindeer • Silent Night • Silver Bells • The Twelve Days of Christmas • What Child Is This? • What Made the Baby Cry? • Wonderful Christmastime • and more.

_____00240206 ....$14.95

See our website for a complete contents list for each volume:
www.halleonard.com

FOR MORE INFORMATION, SEE YOUR LOCAL MUSIC DEALER,
OR WRITE TO:

HAL•LEONARD®
CORPORATION
7777 W. BLUEMOUND RD. P.O. BOX 13819 MILWAUKEE, WI 53213

Prices, contents and availability subject to change without notice.

More Collections from The Lyric Library

More Collections from The Lyric Library

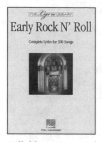

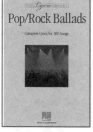